Cambridge Elements

Elements in American Politics
edited by
Frances Lee

RED, GREEN, AND BLUE

The Partisan Divide on Environmental Issues

David Karol
University of Maryland, College Park

CAMBRIDGE
UNIVERSITY PRESS

CAMBRIDGE
UNIVERSITY PRESS

University Printing House, Cambridge CB2 8BS, United Kingdom

One Liberty Plaza, 20th Floor, New York, NY 10006, USA

477 Williamstown Road, Port Melbourne, VIC 3207, Australia

314–321, 3rd Floor, Plot 3, Splendor Forum, Jasola District Centre, New Delhi – 110025, India

79 Anson Road, #06-04/06, Singapore 079906

Cambridge University Press is part of the University of Cambridge.

It furthers the University's mission by disseminating knowledge in the pursuit of education, learning, and research at the highest international levels of excellence.

www.cambridge.org
Information on this title: www.cambridge.org/9781108716499
DOI: 10.1017/9781108673266

First published 2019

A catalogue record for this publication is available from the British Library.

ISBN 978-1-108-71649-9 Paperback
ISBN 978-1-108-67326-6 Online
ISSN 2515-1592 print
ISSN 2515-1606 online

Red, Green, and Blue

The Partisan Divide on Environmental Issues

Elements in American Politics

DOI: 10.1017/9781108673266
First published online: May 2019

David Karol
University of Maryland

Abstract: This Element explores the growth of party divisions on the environment in the United States. It draws on many data sources including Congressional and state legislative voting, campaign contributions, interest group ratings of legislators, party platforms, presidential nominees' speeches, news coverage, and archives.

This study not only adds a case to the party position change literature, but contributes theory by highlighting the changing role of legislators' personal characteristics as an issue polarizes and by showing how interest groups like environmentalists both change party coalitions and are changed by participating in them. It concludes with discussion of how the current party alignment on the environment might change.

This title is also available as Open Access on Cambridge Core at doi.org/ 10.1017/9781108673266

Keywords: parties, environment, political coalitions, United States

Isbns: 978-1-108-71649-9 (PB), 978-1-108-67326-6 (OC)
Issns: 2515-1606 (online), 2515-1592 (print)

Contents

The president most strongly associated with conservation is Theodore Roosevelt. In the first decade of the twentieth century, Roosevelt established the US Forest Service, created several national parks, and signed the Antiquities Act, which he and his successors used to protect many remarkable natural settings. In the later part of the twentieth century, as new challenges emerged, Richard Nixon established the Environmental Protection Agency and signed the Endangered Species Act. Both Roosevelt and Nixon were Republicans, and the environment was not a partisan issue in their time. Yet today Republicans are associated with hostility to environmental regulation, and the issue is prominent in party competition. How did this change occur?

In this Element, I explore the growing party divide on environmental issues in the United States. Understanding the roots of this division is interesting in its own right, but it may also reveal how environmental politics might change again. This is a key question since even in this polarized era few major laws are enacted entirely by one party (Curry and Lee, 2019). A crack in the wall of partisanship on the environment may be needed to address climate change in a serious way.

Exploration of this case also contributes to broader understanding of party interest-group relations and party policies. This Element makes both theoretical and empirical contributions to the literature on issue evolution and party position change. Environmental politics have been largely unexplored by party scholars, although the partisan divide has received some attention from environmental specialists.

This brief Element is not a history of American environmentalism or environmental policy, although it touches on those topics. Rather it is an exploration and analysis of the partisan divide on the environment that has arisen in the United States. This study is distinctive in multiple ways. The examination of state-level as well as national developments is unusual in this literature. I show how environmental groups have become more sensitive to the concerns of racial minorities as they have been incorporated in the Democratic Party and how they in turn have influenced other party-aligned interest groups such as labor unions. Finally, this Element highlights the importance of legislators' personal characteristics for their position-taking on new issues not yet assimilated to party conflict, and their declining significance as the evolution of party coalitions changes politicians' incentives. These dynamics are not explored in most studies of party position change.

1 Plan of the Element

The Element is organized as follows. First I discuss the rise of environmentalism, putting the growing partisan divisions into theoretical perspective, offering comparisons with other issue divides in the United States and with environmental politics in other countries. I then trace the growth of the partisan divide on the environment in platforms, presidential nominees' acceptance speeches, and Congressional voting patterns. I examine the changes in parties' geographical bases and constituency factors in Congress and the importance of conversion and turnover among legislators. I reveal the declining importance of personal characteristics of members of Congress other than party affiliation, even those such as age and education, which remain key predictors of voters' views on the environment. I reveal increasingly partisan patterns of campaign contributions by both environmentalists and industries with which they are in conflict. I chart public opinion, revealing a growing partisan divide on the environment among voters. Turning to the state level, I reveal much variation in the strength of partisan divisions on the environment in statehouses. Not only has the parties' relationship with environmentalism changed; the movement itself has evolved. I cover the transition from "conservationists" to "environmentalists" and the latter's turn against nuclear power. I highlight the growing links between environmentalists and other groups in the Democrats' coalition, which have affected the positions taken by all participants. These lobbies now work together on judicial nominations, which historically did not interest environmentalists. I also discuss developments in the Republican Party, including the mobilization of interests opposed to regulation, and the rejection of environmentalism by religious-right leaders.

Having described the growth in partisan divisions on the environment, I explore possible sources of change, noting the Republicans' dependence on constituencies in demographic decline including older whites, evangelicals, and the fossil fuel sector. I consider GOP elected officials' incentives to revisit policy stands and focus on the recently founded bipartisan Climate Solutions Caucus.

2 The Rise of Environmentalism in the United States

Environmentalism is a relatively new political issue, historically speaking. In the 1910s the question of "conservation" was briefly prominent in the fight between progressive Republicans led by Theodore Roosevelt and the GOP "Old Guard" allied with William Howard Taft (Richardson 1958). Yet the conservation controversy did not endure. Some of conservationists' goals, including expert management of public lands and preservation of scenic locales, became widely accepted. In subsequent decades, environmental issues as we now understand them were largely absent from national debates and party competition.

Policies affecting human exploitation of the natural world have always existed. Yet decisions that many would now view through the prism of environmental concerns, such as whether the government should build dams or nuclear power plants, were instead seen in the mid-twentieth century as questions about the role of the state versus the private sector (Wildavsky 1962). The value of the underlying projects was seldom disputed in the era of "high modernism" (Scott 1999), when many agreed that bigger was better, differing only over whether planning by "big government" or "big business" was best. Republicans took some positions that conservationists approved (sometimes in retrospect), as when they blocked a Bureau of Reclamation plan supported by Democrats in the 1950s to build the Hells Canyon High Dam. This project would have been the world's largest dam on the Snake River in Idaho, flooding a vast area. Private utilities eventually built smaller dams (Brooks 2009).

Similarly, the dispute over "tidelands oil" was a major issue in the 1952 US presidential election. Yet the question was not – as it might be today – whether offshore drilling should be permitted, but rather whether the states or federal government should collect the revenue from oil leases. Most Democrats – especially those from outside the tidelands states like Texas and Louisiana – favored federal control. Republicans advocated states' rights, the position favored by oil interests (Harris 1953).

Environmental consciousness grew in the 1960s and early 1970s. Key milestones included the publication of *Silent Spring* by Rachel Carson in 1962 and celebration of the first Earth Day in 1970. Environmental organizations expanded and multiplied during this period. New groups, including the League of Conservation Voters, Friends of the Earth, and the Natural Resources Defense Council, arose while the membership of older organizations like the Sierra Club greatly expanded. The Club, which had no chapters outside California until the 1950s, had only 10,000 members in 1956, but reached 200,000 by 1981.[1] The Washington presence of environmental organizations and their role in elections correspondingly increased (Mitchell, Mertig, and Dunlap 1991.)

A thorough account of the rise of environmentalism is beyond the scope of this Element, but a few points may be noted. This development was not unique to the United States, but rather occurred throughout the industrialized world. Visible pollution (e.g., the mid-twentieth-century smog in Los Angeles and the fire at the Cuyahoga River in Cleveland) was a factor. A leading account stresses the rise of "postmaterialist" values in societies that have experienced peace and prosperity for generations (Inglehart 1995). Once basic needs are

---

[1] "History: Sierra Club Timeline" http://vault.sierraclub.org/history/timeline.aspx

met, quality of life becomes more salient, and environmentalism is one expression of this.

3 The Growing Party Divide on Environmentalism in Theoretical Context

Environmentalism became a political cause and has increasingly become a partisan one. It is not unique in this respect. Parties have taken up new positions on many issues. This phenomenon and its relationship to changes in party coalitions have long interested scholars. At one time students of parties spoke of "realignments" (Burnham 1970, Sundquist 1983). More recently, as the realignment paradigm has been challenged (Mayhew 2004), scholars have discussed "issue evolution" and "party position change" (Carmines and Stimson 1989, Adams 1997, Wolbrecht 2000, Karol 2009, Wolbrecht and Hartney 2014, Schlozman 2015, Baylor 2018).

The relatively recent emergence of the environmental issue contrasts with questions like trade policy or race, which have been contested since colonial days. Other issues, such as the regulation of labor unions, have been debated for over a century. In this sense, the politics of the environment resembles debates over "social issues" like gun control, abortion, and lesbian, gay, bisexual, and transgender (LGBT) rights. Like environmentalism, these issues arose in the 1960s, when polarization was at its nadir. Initially, these new issues divided elected officials and voters along regional or religious lines at least as much as party ones.

From the 1970s onward, the parties have gradually absorbed these new issues and the constituencies focused on them. These conflicts have not replaced controversies that arose during the New Deal era. Democrats and Republicans still disagree on topics like labor regulation, taxation, and the welfare state. These newer debates, including environmental policy, have supplemented rather than replaced the older controversies in a process Layman et al. (2010) call "conflict extension."

When a new issue arises, a partisan divide is not the only possibility. Reformers may win over elected officials in both parties and achieve victory for their cause, eventually removing it from public debate. Women's suffrage is an example. After decades of struggle, suffragists won a decisive victory and their cause is no longer controversial. An issue may also remain on the political agenda for an extended period before being settled, but cut across party lines the entire time. A prominent example is "the liquor question." Supporters of Prohibition (or "drys") and opponents (or "wets") were numerous in both parties. Republicans were more supportive of Prohibition on average, but the issue split both parties until it disappeared from the national debate with the ratification of the Twenty-second Amendment in 1933 (Poole and Rosenthal 2007, McGirr 2015).

Yet since environmentalism encompasses many policies, it seems unlikely that it could ever be "settled" the way women's suffrage or Prohibition were. At most we might see certain policies, e.g., the existence of some national parks, become uncontroversial.

A new issue can also give rise to new parties. In many countries, the growth of environmental consciousness produced important Green parties that won seats in legislatures and cabinets. There have been new issue-based parties in the United States going back to the nineteenth century when antislavery, populism, and Prohibition all gave rise to parties. Yet significant third parties have been short-lived. As Richard Hofstadter (1955, 97) wrote, in America "third parties are like bees. Once they have stung they die." American electoral institutions discourage the formation of new parties. Although there is a Green Party in the United States, it is less focused on environmental concerns than its name suggests, and it has never won a Congressional seat or electoral vote.

In the early 1970s, party elites gave mixed signals on the environment. Richard Nixon was not a hero of environmentalists, but he signed major legislation including the National Environmental Policy Act and the Endangered Species Act, and oversaw the creation of the Environmental Protection Agency and the National Oceanic Atmospheric Administration. Nixon's advocacy for these reforms – which won massive support in Congress – has been seen as opportunistic, and he later criticized environmentalists (Flippen 2000). Nonetheless, his actions showed that both parties initially sought to address public concerns about the environment.

Nixon's positioning differed from that of later Republican presidents. On this issue, as on many others, Ronald Reagan was the key figure in defining party differences.[2] Reagan allied with the pro-development western "Sagebrush Rebellion," telling a crowd, "Count me in as a rebel."[3] Platforms also showed a growing partisan divide on the issue (Kamienicki 1995). Since then the party division on the environment in the United States has continued to grow.

Why has this happened? I argue that the nature of pre-existing party coalitions made it likely that, once the modern environmental movement arose, it would be drawn into the party system. My coauthors and I (Cohen et al. 2008, Bawn et al. 2012) have argued that parties are best understood as coalitions of "intense

---

[2] Reagan was also the first GOP presidential candidate to win the NRA's endorsement, the first to oppose the ERA, and is credited with identifying Republicans decisively with the pro-life cause (Adams 1997, Karol 2009).

[3] "Reagan Joins Rebels Against Government Ownership of Land," *Miami News* July 5, 1980, p. 28.

policy demanders." The composition of those coalitions evolves, and so do the parties' policy stands. In Karol (2009) I developed three models of change: coalition maintenance, in which politicians modify their positions on issues to appease existing elements of their party's base; coalition group incorporation, in which they take new stands in hopes of bringing targeted constituencies into their party; and coalition expansion, in which elected officials try to win over the public more broadly on issues that lack organized, focused groups.

The different models of change are associated with different rates of reorientation on the part of politicians and different extents to which turnover or conversion by incumbents is the mechanism altering party elites' stands. Group incorporation requires politicians to build new relationships. Typically, some entrenched incumbents do not embrace newcomers to their party. Thus the full transformation of the party requires turnover among party officialdom and is more gradual than coalition maintenance.

The process of environmental group's movement into the Democratic Party is a case of group incorporation, while the Republican rejection of environmentalism is primarily coalition maintenance, although elements of the GOP base have been organized and newly mobilized in ways that make the group incorporation model partially applicable as well.

Environmentalists are mostly in conflict with business interests. Depending on the issue in question they may face off against loggers, agribusiness, utilities, automakers, or other manufacturers. By far their most important conflict in the era of climate change is with fossil fuel producers. All of these economic interests are broadly aligned with the Republican Party. Importantly, that alignment predates the rise of environmentalism. The business community has been Republican-leaning since the days of Abraham Lincoln, when GOP support for the tariff brought manufacturers into the fold. Democrats, once a primarily agrarian party, were eventually more receptive to labor unions when they arose as a political force long before environmentalism became an important movement. While Republicans tried to unite business interests and workers behind their protectionist tariff policies, they could not go beyond that, and unions instead became the core constituency of the New Deal–era Democratic Party, a development that itself reinforced business loyalty to Republicans. This alignment meant that it would always be easier for Democratic politicians to adopt policies sought by environmentalists, despite some conflict between the latter and labor unions. This coalitional argument does not explain the exact policy positions taken by the parties; it only suggests that the issue was likely to become partisan and Democrats were apt to emerge as the party more favorable to environmentalists' concerns.

4 US Environmental Politics in Comparative Perspective

Before delving deeper into American environmental politics, it is worth looking at the larger context. Environmentalism is a global phenomenon (Fisher 2004, Hadden 2015). A comparative perspective is useful for both students of American politics and those concerned with environmentalism. It can reveal what is distinctive about environmental politics in the United States and what requires special explanations.

In any comparative analysis, the selection of cases is key. I present comparisons of the United States and its fellow members of the Organization for Economic Cooperation and Development (OECD), an organization of prosperous democratic countries.

Table 1 summarizes the representation of environmentally minded parties in the thirty-five OECD member states. It reveals several facts and places American environmentalists in comparative perspective. Firstly, in most of these countries "Green" parties have won representation in the lower house of parliament. This is true of thirty-one of thirty-six OECD members, the United States not among them. OECD countries in which environmentalists have never been elected to parliament are a small minority: Japan, South Korea, Poland, Turkey, and the United States. Notably, only one of these countries besides the United States – Japan – has been both prosperous and democratic for more than thirty years. In most countries the peak Green representation in parliament has also occurred within the last decade, indicating growing public concern about the environment.

More stringent tests of the political power of Green parties would note not merely their presence in national parliaments but also the share of seats they won, and whether they were represented in the executive branch of government. In fourteen OECD countries Green parties have won more than five percent of seats in at least one parliamentary election. In eleven, they have held executive branch positions. There is overlap between these two groups. The countries falling into both categories can be seen as those where political environmentalism has made greatest headway. They are Belgium, Finland, Germany, Iceland, Latvia, and Sweden. These are all Northern European counties, and with the exception of Latvia, all states that have been wealthy democracies for many decades.

While America's outlier status among these "peer" countries is notable, it must be qualified in some ways. The absence of a significant Green party in the United States is one result of a two-party duopoly that has no true parallel in other OECD countries. In many of these countries, half a dozen or more parties

Table 1 US environmental politics in comparative perspective: OECD
countries

Country	Peak Green Strength in Parliament	Greens Ever in Cabinet?	2018 Environmental Protection Index Rank	EPA Equivalent Created
Australia	1/150 in 2010/2013/ 2016	NO	21	1971
Austria	24/183 in 2013	NO	8	1972
Belgium	19/150 in 1999	YES	15	1975
Canada	1/338 in 2011/2015	NO	25	1971
Chile	1/155 in 2017	NO	84	2010
Czech Rep.	6/200 in 2006	YES	33	1993
Denmark	9/175 in 2015	NO	3	1971
Estonia	6/101 in 2007	NO	48	1989
Finland	15/200 in 2007/2015	YES	10	1983
France	18/577 in 2012	YES	2	1971
Germany	68/622 in 2009	YES	13	1986
Greece	2/300 in 2015	YES	22	1980
Hungary	16/386 in 2010	NO	43	1988
Iceland	14/63 in 2009	YES	11	1990
Ireland	6/166 in 2007	YES	9	1977
Israel	1/120 in 2015	NO	19	1988
Italy	16/630 in 1992	YES	16	1986
Japan	NONE	NO	20	2001
Korea	NONE	NO	60	1994
Latvia	6/100 in 2014	YES	37	1993
Lithuania	4/135 in 1990	NO	29	1994
Luxembourg	7/100 in 2004/2009	NO	7	1974
Mexico	47/500 in 2015	NO	72	1994
Netherlands	14/150 in 2017	NO	18	1971
New Zealand	14/121 in 2011/2017	NO	17	1986
Norway	1/169 in 2013/2017	NO	14	1972
Poland	NONE	NO	50	1972
Portugal	4/230 in 2005	NO	26	1999
Slovakia	4/150 in 1998	NO	28	Unknown
Slovenia	8/80 in 1990	YES	34	1990
Spain	3/350 in 2015/2016	NO	12	1993
Sweden	25/310 in 2010/2014	YES	5	1987
Switzerland	20/200 in 2007	NO	1	1998
Turkey	NONE	NO	109	2011
UK	1/650 in 2015	NO	6	1970
USA	NONE	NONE	27	1970

regularly win seats in the national legislature. Political scientists agree that the number of parties in a country is largely a function of electoral laws. The first-past-the-post single member district (FPP-SMD) system used in the United States along with a president elected without a runoff strongly encourage interest groups and activists to join one of the two major parties. As the table reveals, Canada and the UK, which share the FPP-SMD system (and much else) with the United States, have only minimal representation of Green parties; there is only one Green legislator in each country's House of Commons.

A country may adopt strong environmental protections without the presence of a significant Green party, as the United States has. As environmentalism has been incorporated in left–right divisions (Dalton 2009), left-wing parties in many countries have become more sensitive to environmental concerns. Conversely, a Green party might also enter parliament and still find its concerns marginalized. So how does the United States compare with other countries in terms of policy outcomes? There is no simple answer to this question, but one widely used measure reported in the table is the Environmental Performance Index (EPI), developed by scholars in association with the World Economic Forum.[4] This group ranks the United States 27th out of 180 countries examined in 2018. Thus, in a global perspective the United States ranks relatively high.

Yet the most appropriate comparison group for the United States is not countries mired in poverty and war, or states with poorly educated populations living under dictatorships. Of the twenty-six countries with higher EPI rankings than the United States, twenty-three are OECD members. So, by this measure the United States scores well below average among peer countries, although it is still highly rated in some categories and subcategories.[5] The relative position of the United States has changed little in recent years. Notably it was in 26th place in the rankings released in January 2016, before Donald Trump became President.[6]

The United States stands out the most on the question of climate change. It is the only country to withdraw from the Paris Agreement and the only OECD country not to have ratified the agreement other than Turkey, which – unlike the United States – remains a signatory.

Yet if the United States now lags its peers on key environmental concerns, this was not always true. Indeed, the United States was long an environmental

---

[4] https://epi.envirocenter.yale.edu/epi-topline?country=&order=field_epi_score_new&sort=desc
[5] The country EPI scores were based on ratings of several policy categories. The United States received its best scores for Sustainable Agriculture (2nd place) and Air Quality (10th place). Conversely, the United States got low ratings for Climate and Energy (114th place) and Biodiversity and Habitat (103rd place).
[6] http://epi2016.yale.edu/sites/default/files/2016EPI_Full_Report_opt.pdf

leader. There is some debate over what constitutes the first "national park," but it is widely accepted that with the creation of Yosemite and Yellowstone National Parks in the nineteenth century and the protection of many other areas under the 1906 Antiquities Act, the United States was a pioneer in wilderness protection. This remained true for much of the twentieth century. In establishing the Environmental Protection Administration in 1970, the United States was among the first countries to create a national agency or department focused on pollution.

While the United States is an outlier in rejecting the Paris Agreement, there is resistance to efforts to address climate change among conservative parties in some other OECD countries. Two countries that often seem to have the most in common with the United States are interesting cases in point. Both Canada and Australia are more economically dependent on natural resources than most advanced industrialized countries. In both nations the leading conservative parties are wobbly on the question of climate change, if not to the extent of the Republican Party. The Canadian Conservative Party, currently in the opposition, supported the Liberal government's entry into the Paris Agreement in 2017, but it insists that Canada can meet its emission reduction targets without imposing a carbon tax.[7] In Australia the governing Liberal Party was hostile to policies geared toward addressing climate change until Malcolm Turnbull became party leader and Prime Minister. Turnbull led Australia into the Paris Agreement. Yet faced with a serious challenge to his leadership from within his parliamentary caucus in August 2018, Turnbull agreed that Australia would not meet its emission targets. He was still deposed only days later.[8]

In other OECD members, leading conservative parties accept the reality of climate change and the need to address it. However, in these countries the same electoral rules that made it possible for Green parties to arise have also allowed for the emergence of right-wing populist parties. While these new groupings tend to focus on immigration, they are often also protectionist, antiestablishment, and hostile to global governance regimes. One manifestation of this is denialist or "skeptical" views on climate change. Prominent examples include the Alternative for Germany and the UK Independence Party, but resistance to policies addressing climate change is common among right-wing populist parties (Lockwood 2018). In the American two-party system, those hostile toward efforts to address climate change are drawn into the Republican Party.

---

[7] "Trudeau's Tough Climate Policies Face a Mounting Backlash," *Bloomberg.com,* July 20, 2018.
[8] "Malcolm Turnbull Removes all Climate Change Targets from Energy Policy in Fresh Bid to Save Leadership," *Sydney Morning Herald,* August 20, 2018; "Australian Prime Minister Ousted in Dispute over Greenhouse Gas Emissions," *Washington Post,* August 24, 2018.

The GOP is the shared, if sometimes uncomfortable home of "populist" and "establishment" conservatives who are in separate parties in other countries with different electoral systems.

5 Charting the Partisan Divide on the Environment

However, while the dominance of two parties has been a near-constant in American politics, their division on environmental matters is far more recent. In order to show the trend in party positioning on the environment, I turn to evidence from party platforms, Presidential nominees' speeches, and Congress. Notably, in all these venues and media – unlike the White House – both parties are always represented.

5.1 Evidence from Platforms and Nominees' Acceptance Speeches

Congress is not the only place to observe the evolution of party positioning. In fact, roll calls have some limitations for that purpose. MCs (Members of Congress) cannot vote on a measure unless it is brought up for debate and the majority party dominates the legislative agenda. This is especially true in the House of Representatives, but increasingly in the Senate as well. Legislative leaders seek to block bills that will divide their caucuses in order to avoid muddying their parties' images, to shield their members from tough votes, and to forestall defeat. Some blocked bills might make the parties appear more or less polarized if they reached the agenda. MCs interested in "position-taking" (Mayhew 1974) also sponsor or cosponsor bills as a way of signaling their positions. These actions are less visible, however, and while abstention among MCs is rare, there is far more variation in sponsorship and cosponsorship, making it difficult to use these behaviors to gauge party positioning. Examination of votes in an issue area allows for exploration of trends in the positioning of parties and individual legislators. Yet it has its limitations.

To more fully understand party positioning on the environment, I turn to an exploration of party platforms and the acceptance speeches of Presidential nominees. These two forms of communication differ in some ways, but unlike the Congressional voting record, they allow a party to fully convey its own messages.

Figure 1 charts the share of Democratic and Republican Party platforms that are on net supportive of a federal role in environmental protection. If a platform includes more verbiage calling for a reduced federal role in this area, the net support percentage could be a negative number, even if some statements favorable to environmental protection are included. I report percentages because platforms

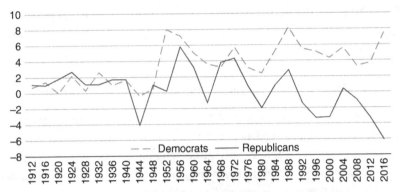

Figure 1 Net support (in percent) for federal role in environmental protection in party platforms: 1912–2016

have grown enormously. The 1916 Republican platform was 2,377 words. The 2004 GOP platform was 41,263 words! A similar trend is evident in Democratic platforms. So simply reporting word counts of language relating to the environment would not reveal emphasis.

The chart reveals several points. In the first half of the twentieth century, "conservation" was not a major focus for either party, although both Democrats and Republicans were on balance supportive of it in most years. In some years Republicans were actually more focused on conservation than Democrats, but the partisan divide was not striking or consistent.

Starting in the middle of the last century, emphasis on this issue increased. While both parties initially showed greater concern for the environment, by the 1970s the current divide began to emerge. From 1972 onward, Democrats consistently offered more net support for a federal role in conservation or environmental protection than Republicans, and the gap between the parties generally grew. In most recent years GOP platforms have been on balance critical of federal efforts to protect the environment. This was true of seven of the ten Republican platforms since Ronald Reagan was nominated in 1980. Prior to that campaign the GOP had been hostile to federal environmental protection efforts only in 1964 and 1944 and the Democrats were so only by the narrowest of margins in 1944.

While less widely studied than party platforms, presidential nominees' acceptance speeches also merit attention. They are, after Presidential debates (which did not occur regularly until 1976), the moment when a party's nominee reaches the largest audience. Unlike platforms, which are read by few and drafted mostly to please the party faithful, convention speeches are written for a broader audience. While partisans are far more likely to view convention speeches, candidates also attempt to reach undecided voters.

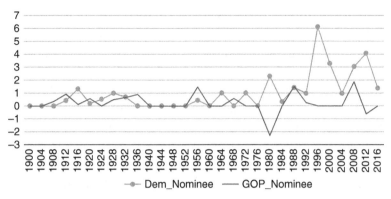

Figure 2 Net support (in percent) for environmental regulation in presidential nominees' speeches: 1900–2016

In addition, while there is no upper bound on platform length, the fact that speeches are televised (and were broadcast on radio before that) informally limits their length. A concern about losing the audience means that space in a speech is at a premium. So the speech not only signals which messages a nominee thinks are best for a broad audience, but which ones are priorities for the campaign.

Figure 2 shows the share of major party presidential nominees' speeches dedicated to the environment. As in the case of platforms, language is coded as positive or negative toward the idea that the federal government should act to protect the environment. Greater numbers indicate that a larger share of the speech was dedicated to supporting a federal role in environmental protection. A negative number correspondingly indicates that the nominee spoke against such regulation. The figure reported is the net balance of supportive words minus critical words. However, in only three cases were nominees at all critical of environmental protection.

The figure reveals several important points. After not being mentioned in 1900 and 1904, the issue of "conservation" was referenced in most speeches during the 1910s and 1920s. These mentions were typically brief, however. No clear distinction between Democrats and Republicans is evident. Reading the speeches reveals brief platitudinous mentions of the value of conservation. Beyond touching this base, nominees stressed that conservation went hand in hand with economic development.

The figure also shows that in the middle of the twentieth century neither party's nominees addressed the issue at all. Starting in 1956, discussion of conservation returned, but in a minimal way, and, as in the earlier period, great party differences were not apparent. In 1956 Adlai Stevenson limited himself to one sentence, while Dwight Eisenhower said just a bit more and focused solely on soil conservation. In the 1960s and 1970s neither party's nominees consistently addressed the environment. When they did so, they devoted no more than a sentence to it.

Yet in recent decades a clearer contrast between the parties on the environment has emerged. Every Democratic presidential nominee since 1980 has addressed the issue. Their remarks have consistently favored environmental regulation and a growing emphasis on this issue is evident. While Al Gore is associated with environmentalism, Bill Clinton in 1996 and Barack Obama in both 2008 and 2012 actually devoted greater shares of their remarks to the topic. Hillary Clinton focused less on the environmental issues than her husband or Obama, but still gave them more attention than most previous nominees had.

The behavior of recent GOP nominees has been more varied, and increasingly distinct from that of their Democratic rivals. Most recent Republican candidates have not discussed the environment in convention speeches, even as Democrats have devoted more attention to it. This was true of Ronald Reagan in 1984, Bob Dole in 1996, George W. Bush in 2000 and 2004, and Donald Trump in 2016. It is also notable that the only two cases in which a nominee's remarks were on balance hostile to environmental regulation were Republicans during this period.[9] In 1980 Reagan was critical of environmental regulations, as was Mitt Romney in 2012. Both nominees asserted that excessive regulation would impair energy production and economic growth.

Comparing the trends in discussion of the environment in party platforms and presidential nominees' speeches reveals some important differences, especially on the Republican side. While many recent GOP nominees have not mentioned the issue in their speeches, it has always been addressed at length in Republican platforms. This suggests that Republican leaders see their pro-development, anti-regulation position as appealing to core constituencies, but less saleable to a broader public.

5.2 Party Position Change on the Environment in Congress

While the Presidential elections that inspire platforms and lead to the selection of nominees who give speeches occur only quadrennially, Congress is always with us. In this arena both Democratic and Republican legislators are given many chances to define their position on environmental issues every year.

---

[9] In 1912 Woodrow Wilson also noted that conservation measures could go too far, but most of his remarks still were supportive of them.

Studying Congress also offers opportunities that exploration of platforms and speeches does not. Since Congress is famously a "they" not an "it," we can not only observe the divide between Democrats and Republicans but explore differences among individual MCs within each party. This in turn helps reveal the dynamics of party position change.

Below I present Figures 3 and 4 showing the distribution of League of Conservation Voters (LCV) ratings among senators and representatives. The League has rated MCs from 0 to 100 since 1972. The ratings are based

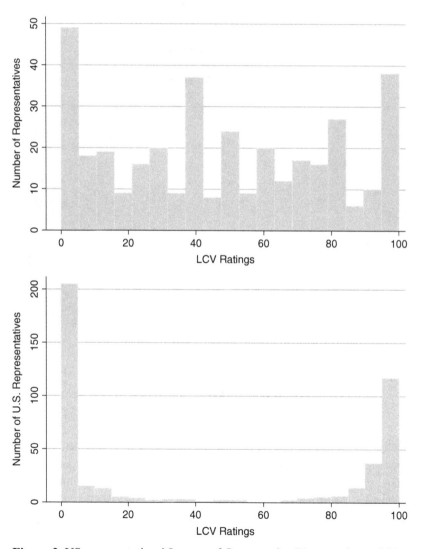

Figure 3 US representatives' League of Conservation Voters ratings of 91st and 115th Congresses (top: 1969–1970; bottom: 2015–2016)

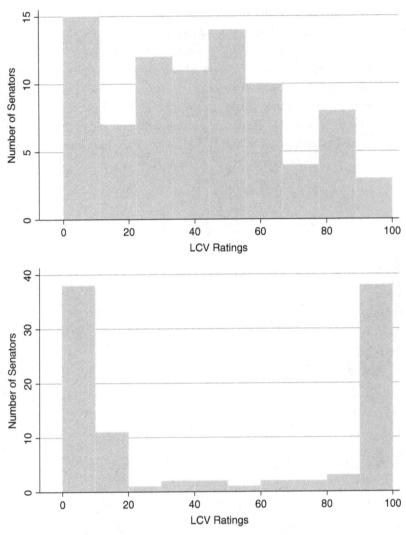

Figure 4 US senators' League of Conservation Voters ratings of 91st and 115th Congresses (top: 1969–1970; bottom: 2015–2016)

chiefly on floor votes.[10] On occasion the League double-weighted important votes and counted cosponsorship of bills and signing discharge petitions and letters. (These alternative measures were used when important bills did not reach the floor of the House or Senate for a vote.) The figures illustrate the change that has occurred via a focus on the 91st Congress (1969–1970), the first rated by the LCV, and the 114th Congress (2015–2016).

---

[10] Scorecards are available at http://scorecard.lcv.org/scorecard/archive

The charts reveal that when Congress first faced the modern controversy over environmental regulation, legislators responded in various ways. Most MCs in the 91st Congress (1969–1970), the first rated by the LCV, were not consistent friends or foes of environmentalists. Instead, the majority compiled mixed records, sometimes siding with the LCV on legislation, and sometimes opposing it.

By the 114th Congress, the picture was very different and revealed a bimodal distribution of ratings. Most MCs now receive a very high or low score from the LCV. This is not merely a story of the "sorting" of environmentalists and their opponents into the two parties. Rather, MCs polarized on environmental issues along partisan lines. Figure 5 depicts the changing association between party affiliation and LCV ratings since their inception. I report the difference between the Democratic and Republican mean LCV score, so positive values indicate greater Democratic support for environmentalism.

A few facts are apparent from the figure. First, from the beginning, Democrats were more supportive of the environmentalists' agenda on average than Republicans. This contrasted with other new issues such as abortion and gun control, on which the party divide was initially minimal.

However, the difference between the party means on environmental issues was initially small. Many Democratic MCs, especially those from the south and west, voted against the wishes of the LCV, while more than a few Republicans, chiefly northeastern moderates, took LCV-approved positions. Second, the parties are now polarized on the environment, much as they are on other issues. This shift was quite gradual. Finally, the same pattern is evident in both the House and the Senate.

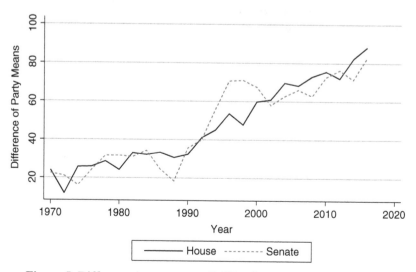

Figure 5 Difference in party mean LCV rating, US House and Senate
(Democratic mean − Republican mean)

Red, Green, and Blue

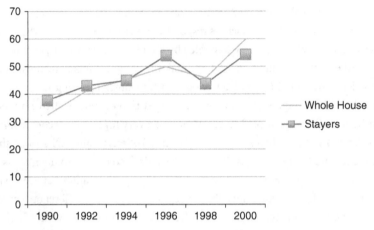

Figure 6 Interparty difference in mean LCV ratings, US House of
Representatives, 1989–2000, whole House and representatives serving
continuously ("stayers") compared

5.3 Conversion and Turnover in Congress and Environmental Polarization

A chart like the one above revealing change in a large body over decades
inevitably prompts questions about the mechanism underlying change. Almost
no legislators have served throughout the entire period depicted. It is possible then
that turnover is the key factor. Conversely, adaptation on the part of continuing
MCs may be at work. One way to explore the question of the roles of turnover and
adaptation by continuing MCs is to compare the positions taken by a group of
long-serving legislators at a time when party positioning is evolving. In Figure 6
I present findings covering a period when the party divisions on the environment
in Congress were growing more rapidly than they did in earlier or more recent
years. Just under one-third of seats were held by the same representatives
throughout this period. These are represented as "stayers" in the figure.[11]

The figure reveals only modest differences between the trend evident among
the minority of MCs present throughout the period depicted and developments in
the whole House. Among stayers the party divide on the environment is slightly
greater at the beginning of the period and slightly smaller at the end. This finding
suggests some inertia in MCs' issue positioning, meaning that turnover may
heighten divisions between the parties. The slightly greater party division among

---

[11] A small number of legislators present at the beginning and end of the period, but who did not
serve continuously, are not counted as stayers.

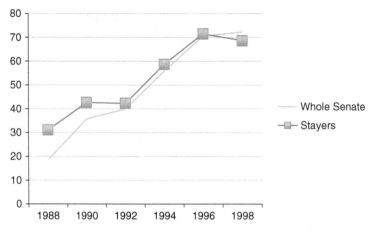

Figure 7 Interparty difference in mean LCV ratings, US Senate, 1987–1998, whole Senate and senators serving continuously ("stayers") compared

the stayers at the beginning of the period could reflect the fact that they tend to represent safer seats, a characteristic associated with greater party line voting.

Yet the more dramatic finding evident in the figure is that long-serving MCs did adapt. The same pattern is evident among them and the whole House. Thus conversion or adaptation contributed to the growing party polarization on environmental issues in the US House of Representatives during the 1990s.

Figure 7 depicts a similar comparison for the Senate. Since there is a large increase evident in the party divide in the upper house of Congress a bit sooner, I start the analysis one Congress earlier than I do for the House and end it one Congress earlier as well. For the most part, I am examining the same period in both chambers.

The pattern in the Senate is broadly similar to that observed in the House. There is a great increase in party divisions on environmental issues from the late 1980s to the late 1990s. This trend is visible among senators serving throughout this period and in the Senate as a whole. To a slightly greater extent than in the House, differences are evident between the long-serving legislators and the rest of the chamber. Greater partisan divisions among stayers are evident at the beginning of the period. However, by the end of the period observed, the gap between Democratic and Republican stayers is slightly smaller than it is among senators generally. This suggests, even more clearly than the findings among representatives, some stickiness in the positions of continuing legislators. This may reflect the gradual incorporation of groups in party coalitions: environmentalists in the Democratic Party and energy interests in the Republican Party. Entrenched MCs may be reelected for a time without accommodating new party constituencies (Karol 2009). Yet the main story is one of adaptation by Members of Congress.

5.4 Polarization of Congressional Leaders
on Environmentalism

Another way to observe the change in parties' positioning on environmental issues is to focus on leaders. Congressional leaders are the most visible political figures beyond the President and Vice President. When a party does not control the White House, Congressional leaders are its public face. So it is worth examining leaders at the dawn of modern environmental politics and more recently. In Table 2 I report LCV scores for party leaders in the first two Congresses rated by the group (the 91st and 92nd) and the two most recent ones for which complete LCV scores are available (the 113th and 114th). In some cases, there was leadership turnover between one Congress and the next.

The table reveals that even party leaders were not polarized on environmental issues at first. Most had middling LCV ratings, and there was overlap between the two parties. Remarkably, the Democratic Senate Majority Leader, Mike Mansfield of Montana, had a lower rating in the 91st Congress than the Republican Minority Leader, Hugh Scott of Pennsylvania. The Republican Whip's rating (Robert Griffin of Michigan) was similar to Mansfield's and higher than that of his Democratic counterpart, Robert Byrd of West Virginia, who replaced Edward Kennedy as Democratic Whip in the 92nd Congress.

In the House, typically the more partisan chamber, there was only slightly greater evidence of a party divide. (There is no rating for the Speaker, who by custom seldom votes.) Both Democratic leaders in the 91st Congress – Majority Leader Carl Albert of Oklahoma and Majority Whip Hale Boggs of Louisiana – represented oil-producing states and received middling to low scores from the LCV. Their ratings were higher than those of House Minority Leader Gerald Ford of Michigan and Minority Whip Les Arends of Illinois, but none of the leaders in the 91st Congress were very supportive of the LCV's positions. In the 92nd Congress, Tip O'Neill of Massachusetts became the Majority Whip. He had the highest score of any leader, but still voted with the LCV only 60 percent of the time.

The contrast between the positioning of Congressional leaders on the environment in the early years of the issue and their current alignment is marked. The LCV ratings of leaders in the 113th and 114th Congresses reveal great polarization. There is little variation among Democrats or Republicans, but a large gulf between the parties.

It is notable that the constituencies of the party leaders have changed. Initially, Democratic leaders chiefly represented areas in which resource extraction was important in the local economy. Albert and Boggs were from the "oil patch," and Mansfield and Byrd represented mining states. The same cannot be

Table 2 Congressional leaders' LCV ratings over time

	Leader	91st Congress	92nd Congress	Leader	113th Congress	114th Congress
Senate Majority Leader	Mike Mansfield (D-MT)	27	63	Mitch McConnell (R-KY)	6	5
Senate Majority Whip	Edward Kennedy (D-MA)	71	*	John Cornyn(R-TX)	11	2
Senate Majority Whip	Robert Byrd (D-WV)	*	20	*	*	*
Senate Minority Leader	Hugh Scott (R-PA)	56	26	Harry Reid (D-NV)	94	100
Senate Minority Whip	Robert Griffin (R-MI)	24	59	Dick Durbin (D-IL)	94	100
House Majority Leader	Carl Albert (D-OK)	28		Kevin McCarthy (R-CA)	2	1
House Majority Leader	Hale Boggs (D-LA.)	*	28	*	*	*
House Majority Whip	Hale Boggs (D-LA)	51	*	Steve Scalise (R-LA)	2	1
House Majority Whip	Tip O'Neill (D-MA.)	*	60	*	*	*
House Minority Leader	Gerald Ford (R-MI)	10	20	Nancy Pelosi (D-CA)	90	100
House Minority Whip	Les Arends (R-IL)	0	7.5	Steny Hoyer (D-MD)	87	90

Red, Green, and Blue

Table 3 Evolution of Democratic and Republican constituencies: 92nd and 114th Congresses compared

	Mean Democratic Presidential Vote Share	Southern Share of Party Caucus	Energy & Mining Employment as Share of Population	Farmers as Share of Population
92nd Congress 1971–1972	Democratic 44.8%	Democratic 35.2%	Democratic 0.4%	Democratic 1.8%
	Republican 38.7%	Republican 16.2%	Republican 0.27%	Republican 1.8%
114th Congress 2015–2016	Democratic 64%	Democratic 17.4%	Democratic 0.24%	Democratic 0.4%
	Republican 40.7%	Republican 44.6%	Republican 0.74%	Republican 1.5%

said of Nancy Pelosi and Steny Hoyer, who represent metropolitan districts. Harry Reid and Richard Durbin represented states where mines had been worked, but by the time they reached the Senate leadership, this sector was far less important in their states than it once had been.

This comparison suggests that the geographic realignment of the parties could underlie their polarization on the environment. To investigate that possibility we need to move beyond leaders and look at the constituencies of MCs more generally.

5.5 Changing Partisan Geography in Congress

The growth of the partisan divide on the environment evident among both party leaders and rank and file MCs coincided with a demographic and geographic realignment of the two parties. Many factors beyond environmental debates contributed to this change. Yet whatever their origins, these shifts may have affected the politics of the environment to the extent that MCs are influenced by their constituents. In Table 3, I compare the Democratic and Republican constituencies in the 92nd Congress (1971–1972), the first one for which LCV scores are available for all legislators, and the recent 114th Congress (2015–2016).[12]

In the first Congress, the vote share of the most recent Democratic Presidential nominee (Hubert Humphrey) was only slightly higher in

---

[12] Data are from Census of Agriculture and Professor Scott Adler's Congressional district dataset https://sites.google.com/a/colorado.edu/adler-scott/data/congressional-district-data

Democrats' states and districts than in those of their GOP colleagues. By contrast, in the 114th Congress the gap was enormous. Democratic MCs mostly represented areas President Obama had won easily in 2012, while most Republicans came from constituencies where he lost badly.

Other variables also reveal sharp reversals. In the earlier Congresses, most Southerners were Democrats. Yet Southerners made up a larger share of the Congressional GOP in 2015–2016 than they had of the Senate and House Democrats in 1971–1972. Large-scale change is also evident in the economic bases of the Democrats and Republicans' constituencies. In the 92nd Congress, those working in the energy and mining sector made up a slightly larger share of the constituency of Congressional Democrats. By the 114th Congress, however, the same sector was three times as large a share of Republicans' constituencies compared to Democratic ones. Farmers, who made up an equal share of both parties' constituency in 1971–1972, were nearly four times as great a fraction of GOP MCs' constituencies compared to those of Democrats by 2015–2016.

These shifts are not unrelated. The South was the most rural section of the country, and long the most Democratic region. Yet by 1970, ticket-splitting was common in the South. Southerners frequently rejected Democratic presidential nominees, but still voted for Democratic candidates further down the ballot. Much energy production is located in the historically Democratic states of Texas, Louisiana, and Oklahoma.

The political realignment of white Southerners over the last five decades has reshaped both parties. It was not driven primarily by the politics of environmental regulation. Yet by reshaping party constituencies, this realignment had consequences for the positioning of Democrats and Republicans on environmental issues, helping to polarize them. There are far fewer Democrats and Republicans in Congress today who are cross-pressured on environmental questions than there once were.

The "sorting" of groups of constituents into party coalitions and the changes in partisan geography have been widely noted (Bishop 2008, Hopkins 2017). Yet a closer look reveals that these shifts do *not* fully account for the parties' polarization on environmental issues. To see this, we can examine cases in which Democratic and Republican elected officials face the same constituency. Presidential nominees compete for electoral votes, but have increasingly disagreed on environmental issues. Yet we only observe one President at a time, so we cannot know how different the policies pursued by the losing nominee would have been from those the victor implemented.

A better source of evidence on this point is found in the Senate. At any given time, several states are represented by a senator from each party. These states with "mixed delegations" allow us to see how Democratic and Republican

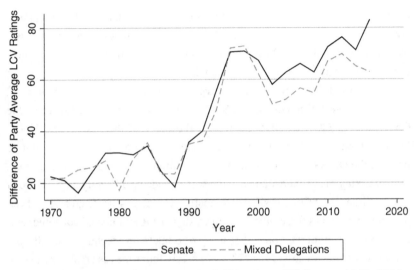

Figure 8 Difference of party average LCV ratings, US Senate: 1969–2016

senators represent the same constituents over time. If the growing partisan divide on the environment stems chiefly from Democrats and Republicans increasingly representing states and districts with different preferences, we would not expect an increasing divide between Democratic and GOP senators in mixed delegations.

Figure 8 reports the difference of party average scores among all senators and among the subset from mixed delegations during that Congress.

The figure reveals that the gap between the parties on environmental issues among senators in mixed delegations is similar to that evident in the Senate as a whole over the five decades charted. In a few Congresses, the partisan divide on environmental issues in the mixed delegation states even exceeded that among all senators. More recently Democrats and Republicans in mixed delegations have been slightly less polarized on environmental issues than the whole senate, as one would expect, but the partisan gap is still growing even among them. This is evidence that the party polarization on environmental issues is not mostly a result of their geographic realignment.

5.6 Members of Congress and the Environment: A Multivariate Analysis

A more precise understanding of the changing relationship among constituency, party, and MCs' positioning on issues requires multivariate analysis. In the following analyses, the dependent variable is MC's LCV ratings. Key independent variables assess the role of party affiliation, constituency, and personal characteristics.

While constituency factors are important, elected officials' personal background and beliefs may matter as well. Politicians are people too, and have beliefs, just like voters. Students of Congress have long seen MCs' personal views as a key factor underlying their behavior (Fenno 1978, Poole 1988). Unlike voters' views however, politicians' stands are public and affect their careers. The importance of legislators' convictions and background may vary as party coalitions evolve and MCs perceive more or less leeway on an issue.

MCs' beliefs are not directly observable, complicating efforts to determine their importance in explaining legislators' behavior. Yet if we find the same associations between MCs' personal characteristics and policy preferences that are evident among survey respondents, we may infer that the politicians are acting on their own beliefs. Many studies show associations between legislators' personal characteristics and their votes.[13] Like all people, their political views are shaped by their racial, religious, gender, and class socialization.

Yet it is often unclear whether the association between MC's personal characteristics and their votes reflects their own views or their ties to a subconstituency (Bishin 2009) including members of the community in question. If an MC views a community with whom she is associated as part of her political base, she may give their preferences extra weight in deciding how to vote, whether or not she privately shares their concerns. In many cases there will be little conflict between the MC's own views and those prevailing in the community in which she was socialized. Yet these two behaviors – acting on conviction and representing others – are analytically distinct, if often hard to differentiate in practice.

Happily, in the case of the environment this is less of a problem. Characteristics associated with environmentalist views – education and age – have not typically delineated party constituencies or voting blocs.[14] People cluster far less geographically on the basis of these characteristics than they do along racial, ethnic, or religious lines. There is also less interest group organization based on these characteristics than there is for many others.[15]

For these reasons, an association between age, level of education, or sex and MCs' positions on the environment is more likely to reflect the connection between these characteristics and legislators' policy views rather than their

---

[13] This claim is investigated in "descriptive representation" studies focused on race (Grose 2011), gender (Swers 2005), religion (McTague and Pearson-Merkowitz 2013), military service (Gelpi and Feaver 2002), and class (Carnes 2013).

[14] Only recently have age and educational attainment become highly associated with voting patterns, with the younger and more highly educated being more supportive of Democrats. These relationships had yet to develop during most of the years I examine in this Element. "Educational Divide in Vote Preferences on Track to Be Wider than in Recent Elections," *FactTank Pew Research Center*, September 15, 2016; "The Generation Gap in American Politics," *Pew Research Center*, March 1, 2018.

[15] To be sure, the AARP is prominent, but other age cohorts are not so organized.

catering to any subconstituency. Surveys have long shown that younger and better-educated respondents are most supportive of environmental regulation. Dunlap and Allen (1976) found this to be true among MCs as well in the 92nd Congress (1971–1972). Yet this relationship has not been investigated in more recent years, even as partisan divisions in Congress have grown.

When issues are new, legislators may be more apt to vote based on their own views, which reflect their backgrounds. MCs mistakenly project their own beliefs onto their constituents (Miller and Stokes 1963, Miler 2010); this may be especially true on newer issues. MCs may also be better informed about the views of constituents with whom they share traits and interact most often. MCs may also favor a "re-election constituency" (Fenno 1978) of voters they see as supporters, or a "prospective constituency" of potential backers (Bishin 2009). Thus, in practice, a Democratic MC and a Republican MC will have different constituencies when representing the same state or district.

MCs may perceive less discretion to vote on the basis of their views as the cues sent from party-aligned interest groups and constituents become clear (Karol and Thurston 2014). As interest groups and activists focus on an issue and "intense policy demanders" (Bawn et al 2012) are drawn into party coalitions, elected officials' incentives change (Karol 2009). Politicians seeking to win nominations and mobilize their base in general elections will take these groups' preferences into account, reducing the importance of factors that might matter more earlier in the history of an issue – including overall constituency attitudes and MCs' personal backgrounds and views.

To understand the changing importance of these factors, I turn to a multivariate analysis of Congressional voting patterns. A positive coefficient is anticipated for the birth year variable, given previous findings that younger MCs and voters are more supportive of environmental regulation. I also include an indicator variable that takes a one if an MC is a woman and a zero otherwise. Following Dunlap and Allen (1976, 393), I code educational attainment among MCs as an interval variable, with zero meaning no college, one denoting matriculation or a community college degree, two standing for a bachelor's degree, three representing a master's degree, four denoting professional degree, and five indicating a doctorate.

The role of education, however, is more complicated than age. MCs are older than the public. While the median age in the United States is 37,[16] the average age of representatives is now 58 and that of senators is 62.[17] Yet, comparing MCs to the voting-age population, and – even more so – actual voters, reveals a smaller gap. In the 2016 election, exit polls revealed that the median voter was in her late 40s.[18] The age range in Congress is great, as it is among voters, so the same measure is appropriate for both groups.

The gap in educational attainment between MCs and the public is more striking. Already in the 91st Congress (1969–1970), the first one for which the LCV released ratings of legislators, 61 percent of representatives and 66 percent of senators had some kind of graduate degree. Only 6.2 percent of representatives and 4.9 percent of senators had not attended college.

By contrast, the Census reported that in 1970 only 21.6 percent of Americans twenty-five or older had spent any time in college and almost 45 percent had not graduated high school.[19] Today's public is better educated than the one that existed in 1970 at the time of the first Earth Day. By 2015, only 12.6 percent of the population twenty-five and over had not graduated high school, and 32.5 percent had at least a college degree.[20] Yet a gap between the public and its representatives persists, since educational attainment has also increased among MCs. By the 114th Congress, 65 percent of representatives and 76 percent of senators had advanced degrees, while just over 5 percent of representatives and, remarkably, all senators were college graduates.

For this reason, I add another education-related variable to analyses besides one measuring educational attainment. This is an indicator variable coded as one if an MC attended an elite college or university at the undergraduate or graduate level (whether or not they received a degree there), and zero otherwise. I coded as elite all Ivy League universities, MIT, Duke, The University of Chicago, Northwestern University, the University of Michigan, UC-Berkeley, Stanford, Cal Tech, the US Military and Naval Academies, and several liberal arts colleges. I also count the University of Virginia and New York University law schools as elite, but not their undergraduate or graduate programs.

In the 91st Congress, 33 percent of representatives and 46 percent of senators had attended one of these elite institutions. By the 114th Congress, the share of MCs having attended these schools had declined to 21 percent in the House and 36 percent in the Senate. I do not have an analogous percentage for the adult population, but it is far lower than the figure for Congress.

Table 4 reports ordinary least squares regression models of MCs' LCV ratings for the 92nd and 114th Congresses.[21] I present two models, one

---

[18] www.cnn.com/election/results/exit-polls
[19] www2.census.gov/programs-surveys/demo/tables/educational-attainment/1970/p20-207/tab-01.pdf
[20] www.census.gov/content/dam/Census/library/publications/2016/demo/p20-578.pdf
[21] I use the 92nd Congress instead of the 91st because the League only reported scores for those Members of the 91st Congress who were still serving in the 92nd.

Table 4 LCV scores in the 92nd Congress (1971–1972) and 114th Congress (2015–2016)
OLS Regression

US House of Representatives			
	92nd Congress	**92nd Congress**	**114th Congress**	**114th Congress**
---	---	---	---	---
Birth Year	0.73(0.13)*	0.67(0.10)*	−0.91(0.18)*	0.04 (0.04)
Education	2.33(0.96)*	1.81(0.72)*	2.07(1.85)	0.28(0.41)
Elite Education	13.33(2.85)*	8.90(2.20)*	29.27(4.89)*	3.36(1.11)*
Woman	24.83(8.22)*	4.21(6.22)	28.06(4.99)*	0.96(1.13)
Energy/ Mining		−3.84(0.89)*		−0.48(0.27)
Farming		−12.5(2.7)*		−0.39(0.28)
South		−12.5(2.7)*		−2.66(0.95)*
Dem. Pres. Vote		83.4(9.2)*		19.7(5.6)*
Democrat		9.56(2.16)*		79.8(1.50)*
Constant	−1366(242.7)*	−1304.5(181.3)*	1811.6(360.5)*	−72.52(82.6)
Adj. R-Sq.	0.17	0.54	0.18	0.96
N	428	428	440	440

US Senate			
	92nd Congress	**92nd Congress**	**114th Congress**	**114th Congress**
---	---	---	---	---
Birth Year	0.83(0.27)*	0.82(0.22)*	−0.59(0.39)	0.04(0.13)
Education	3.67(2.27)	−0.05(1.86)	4.82(4.76)	1.92(1.59)
Elite Education	13.5(5.5)*	10.5(4.5)*	29.2(8.8)*	1.16(3.07)
Woman			37.94(10.1)*	6.77(3.57)
Energy/ Mining		−3.16(1.4)*		−2.44(1.04)*
South		−13.3(6.4)*		−3.97(3.43)
Dem. Pres. Vote		75.9(28.9)*		49.18(22.27)
Democrat		18.45(5.33)*		70(3.89)*
Constant	−1559(521.9)*	−1564.7(507.1)*	1168.2(761.9)	−126.6
Adj. R-Sq.	0.20	0.175	0.175	0.91
N	99	99	100	100

* indicates p-value < 0.05

including variables capturing MCs' personal characteristics, and another in which constituency variables and party affiliation are added. Since there were never more than two women senators until the 103rd Congress (1993–1994), I only include an indicator variable for sex in the House models for the 92nd Congress.

Much change is evident over time. In the 92nd Congress, younger MCs, women, those who were better-educated, and those who had attended an elite college were more supportive of the LCV's positions on the environment. These relationships generally persist in the second model, which includes variables capturing party, the weight of energy and mining in the district economy, the vote share received by the Democratic Presidential nominee, and an indicator variable coded as one if the MC is from the South.

Comparing the recent Congress to the early one reveals important changes. The coefficients for the constituency variables decline, while the party coefficient grows. MCs are voting more along party lines, and their personal characteristics as well as those of their states and districts are less predictive of their stands on environmental issues than they once were, when party affiliation is included in models.

We would like to know how and when the changes shown in the table occurred. Below I present Figures 9 and 10 charting the beta coefficients for the variables included in the models presented for the House and Senate in each successive Congress from 1969 through 2016.

The figures reveal substantial if gradual change in both chambers of Congress. Initially, many factors predict MCs' LCV scores including not only party affiliation, but also age, level of education and sex. Democrats, younger and female legislators, the more highly educated, and those who attended elite universities were more supportive of the environmentalist policy agenda. The demographic variables of age, sex, and educational attainment initially worked the same way among MCs as they did among the public.

Constituency characteristics were also predictive of MCs' votes. Those from constituencies where Democratic presidential nominees fared well, those from northern states, and those representing areas in which energy, mining, and farming were not strong presences in the economy were more supportive of the LCV's positions.

In both chambers, the party coefficient grew over time, indicating a widening partisan divide. By contrast, variables measuring MCs' personal characteristics and their constituencies declined in importance. Most were no longer significant predictors of MCs' votes on environmental issues by the end of the era depicted.

This finding, along with the differentiation between Democratic and Republican presidential candidates on the environment, reveals that the

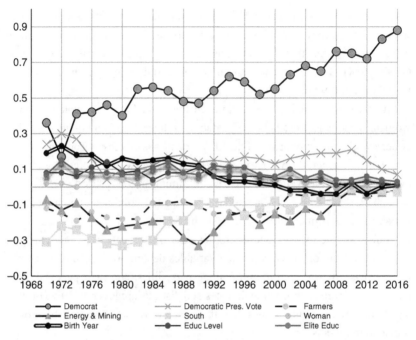

Figure 9 Support for environmentalism, OLS regression beta coefficients, US House of Representatives: 1969–2016

polarization in this policy area is not due only to changes in the geographical constituencies of the parties. Instead, Democratic and Republican presidents and senators have represented the same country and the same states in increasingly different ways. Simplistic notions of elected officials reflecting the preferences of the median voter in their constituencies do not explain these dynamics. To better understand why this is so, I turn to focus on interest groups, campaign finance, and public opinion.

5.7 Party Coalitions, Interest Groups, and Campaign Finance

If Democrats and Republicans represent states and districts in a different way than they used to, changes in their coalitions can help explain this shift. Leading environmental organizations have long been formally nonpartisan. In practice, however, environmentalists have gradually been incorporated in the Democratic coalition.

The Sierra Club and League of Conservation Voters have long favored Democratic candidates. In recent years, newer environmental groups have become prominent. Environment America was founded in 2007. In 2016, the group endorsed Hillary Clinton for president. All eleven of the senate

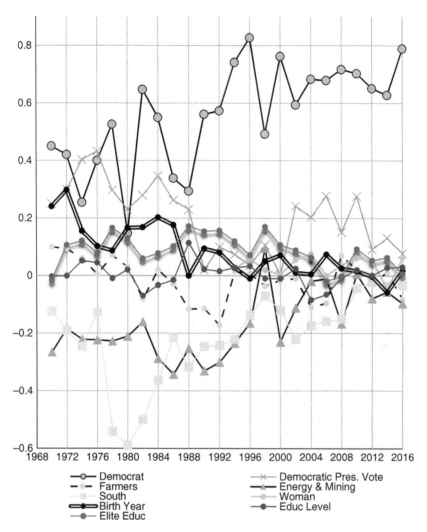

Figure 10 Support for environmentalism, OLS regression beta coefficients, US Senate: 1969–2016

candidates Environment America supported were Democrats, as were 41 of their 45 endorsed candidates for US Representative. The group endorsed four incumbent Republican representatives, none of whom faced strong opposition in 2016.[22]

NextGen America (formerly NextGen Climate Action), founded and largely funded by hedge fund billionaire Tom Steyer, was very active in the 2014 and

---

[22] The endorsees were Frank LoBiondo and Chris Smith of New Jersey, Patrick Meehan of Pennsylvania, and Dave Reichert of Washington. http://environmentamerica.org/page/ame/environment-america-2016-endorsements

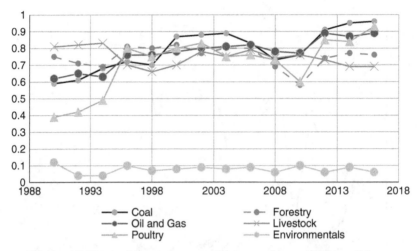

Figure 11 Share of campaign contributions going to GOP candidates: environmentalists and corporate lobbies: 1990–2016

2016 cycles. Eschewing direct contributions to candidates, this organization funded massive independent expenditures favoring Democratic candidates and opposing Republican ones.[23]

Why has this happened? The conflict between environmentalists' policy preferences and those of various elements of the business and farm lobbies has made it easier for Democrats than business-oriented Republicans to take the Green side of issues.[24] In an earlier era, Democrats, then a chiefly agrarian party, were likewise in a better position to incorporate labor unions than a Republican Party already close to business interests.

One way to assess the changing alignment of interest groups and parties is to explore campaign finance data. The Center for Responsive Politics has coded federal campaign contributions since 1990. Using their data, Figure 11 reveals contribution trends not only for environmentalists, but also for economic sectors at odds with them: oil and gas producers, coal companies, livestock and poultry producers, and forestry-related firms.

Unfortunately, industry-level statistics for campaign contributions are not available prior to 1990, when the parties' polarization on environmental issues was already well underway.

Still, important change is visible over the two and a half decades of available data. Already in 1990, environmental groups' contributions overwhelmingly

---

[23] "Financier Plans Big Ad Campaign on Climate Change," *New York Times*, February 17, 2014.
[24] Democratic politicians have also faced conflicts in their coalition between environmentalists and labor unions. Yet these have been episodic in nature, usually focusing on secondary concerns of a minority of declining private-sector unions.

went to Democratic candidates. The data, however, reveal important shifts among corporate lobbies since then. The trend among business sectors concerned with environmental policy has been strongly toward the Republicans. With the exception of poultry producers, who gave only 39 percent of their donations to Republicans in 1990, the sectors charted already favored GOP candidates in the earliest cycle examined. Livestock producers gave 81 percent to Republicans in 1990, while the forestry sector gave 75 percent to the GOP. A smaller imbalance in energy sector contributions was evident, with oil and gas giving 62 percent of its donations to Republicans and coal giving GOP candidates 59 percent.

Since Democrats controlled Congress in the early 1990s, and many business lobbies had pursued an incumbent-friendly "access" strategy, this Republican leaning is notable. For context, data from the Center for Responsive Politics show that commercial banks gave 51 percent of their contributions to Democratic candidates in 1990, 50 percent in 1992, and 49 percent in 1994. Defense contractors, a sector especially dependent on government, directed 53 percent of their contributions to Democrats in 1990, 54 percent in 1992, and 59 percent in 1994. This was the case despite the fact that Democrats had long been less supportive of military spending than Republicans.

Yet while energy and agribusiness donors already leaned Republican in the early 1990s, they have moved overwhelmingly into the GOP camp since then (Karol 2015). Even when Democrats regained control of Congress in 2006, poultry and forestry producers increased contributions to Democrats but still favored GOP candidates. Energy and agribusiness did not revert to the levels of support they had given Democrats during the earlier period of Democratic control that ended in 1994.

Interest groups concerned with environmental regulation reflect clear partisan alignments in their pattern of campaign contributions. As in the case of voters, it is not so easy to disentangle causality. Many scholars see contributions as buying access or attention from officials already supportive of a group's concerns rather than determining MCs' policy positions. Yet to the extent that we accept that donors are a factor in MCs' decisions, these findings can help explain why Democrats and Republicans represent the same districts and states in different ways when it comes to environmental issues.

5.8 Polarization in Public Opinion on Environmental Issues

I now turn to consider partisan divisions on environmental regulation in public opinion. The relationship between voters' policy preferences and the stands taken by elected officials is not straightforward. Much commentary takes voters' views as given and assumes that politicians adapt to please them. When Democratic and Republican voters disagree, attitudes in MCs' districts will differ by party and this will be even truer of primary electorates. Hence, a growing partisan divide on an issue among voters could in principle explain a similar split among elected officials.

Yet elected officials often take positions that are only reflected in public opinion years later, if ever (Zaller 1992). For example, Republican voters were only slightly *more* likely than Democrats to be pro-choice until the mid-1980s (Adams 1997, Karol 2009, 2014), despite the pro-life stands of President Reagan, most GOP MCs, and the 1976 and 1980 Republican Platforms. Republican voters lagged GOP officialdom in embracing pro-life views, so they cannot have driven this change. Lenz (2012) finds much cue taking by voters. Party identification and other group identities are more deeply rooted than issue preferences for most voters (Achen and Bartels 2016). This dynamic appears to be at work in the case of climate change, where mass attitudes have polarized in recent years as Republican elites have downplayed the problem and rejected attempts to address it (McCright and Dunlap 2011).

Yet even if party leaders, especially the President, can sometimes reshape voters' views, that does not make the resulting attitudes irrelevant for individual MCs. Most must accept the distribution of attitudes as given. Voters may use these attitudes to evaluate congressional candidates. If so, the gap between Democratic and Republican voters is another reason besides campaign contributions why MCs of different parties represent the same state or district in different ways on environmental issues.

To assess the relationship between party identification and views on environmental regulation in the public, I turn to the General Social Survey (GSS). Since 1973, it has queried respondents about whether federal spending on environmental protection is "too little," "too much," or "just right." While this question does not capture all environmental policy concerns, there is value in a survey item with stable wording over decades.

The statistic I report is the difference in "net support" for environmental spending among Democratic and Republican partisans. This is the percentage of respondents in each party saying there was "too little" spending minus the share saying there was "too much." I then subtract the Republican net support percentage from the Democratic one. Positive values for the interparty difference in net support indicate that Democratic respondents were more supportive of governmental action to protect the environment.

In Figure 12 I present the trend among two groups of respondents: all partisans, including those who initially define themselves as "independent"

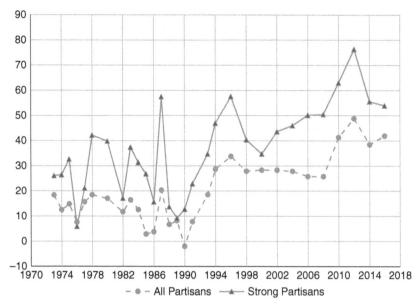

Figure 12 Party difference in support for environmental spending, all partisans and strong partisans, general social survey: 1973–2016

but then concede that they lean toward a party, and the subset that self-identify as "strong" Democrats or Republicans. While there are clear differences between these two groups, the same trend is evident among them.

Starting in 1973, the first year the question was asked, Democratic respondents were more supportive of environmental spending than Republicans. There is short-term fluctuation, but the clear trend is toward a growing divide between Democratic and Republican respondents on the issue. With few exceptions, this gap is notably larger among strong partisans than among all partisan respondents. This is important because the views reported by strong partisans are more likely to be similar to those of the party activists who are disproportionately visible to MCs.

This trend is broadly similar to the one evident among Members of Congress. In both cases an increase in partisan divisions is evident. In both we also observe an early growth followed by a period of oscillation. The trend in Congress is somewhat smoother, with less short-term fluctuation evident than among the public. This may be a function of both the finer grained measure (a rating based on dozens of votes in a single Congress) and the fact that there is limited turnover in Congress in the short term.

Surveys reveal that the importance of party identification for views on the environment has grown vis-à-vis other respondent characteristics. I show this in Table 5 with results from a multivariate analysis. The dependent variable is

Table 5 Support for environmental regulation, OLS regression models: 1996 and 2016 American National Election Studies

	1996	2016
Democrat	0.39(0.05)*	0.83(0.03)*
Age	−0.01(0.002)*	−0.013(0.002)*
Education	0.16(0.03)*	0.07(0.01)*
Woman	−0.08(0.08)	0.17(0.06)*
Constant	4.37(0.22)*	4.40(0.19)*
Adj. R-Sq.	0.08	0.17
N	1345	3265

* = p-value < 0.01

American National Election Study respondents' self-placement on a seven-point scale, with higher values indicating a greater priority on environmental protection as opposed to jobs. This is a finer-grained measure than the GSS spending item and arguably offers a better comparison with the LCV ratings, which range from zero to 100. I report results from 1996, when the ANES first included this question, and from 2016. I present the results of ordinary least squares regression assessing the relationship between respondents' views on the environment and key characteristics shown to be predictors of MCs' positions on the issue: partisanship, age, level of education, and sex.

The doubling of the Democrat coefficient indicates that the association between party and environmental policy views has grown, controlling for demographic variables. Even when party identification is included in the model, respondents' age and level of education are also significant predictors of their self-placement on the scale in the expected ways; younger and more highly educated respondents remain more supportive of environmental regulations. This is also true of female respondents in the second survey.

There are some difficulties in comparing these findings with the voting behavior of MCs. The ANES sample is much larger than the House, let alone the Senate, and statistical significance is in part a function of the number of cases examined. A seven-point scale is also not equivalent to a rating based on many votes in a legislative body. Yet the results show both that the partisan divide on the environment among voters has grown and that the demographics scholars identified as supporting environmental regulation in the 1970s still do, even controlling for party identification.

However, while age and educational attainment remain important predictors of voters' views on the environment, they now matter far less on Capitol Hill.

The weakened association between MCs' personal characteristics and their votes on the environment reflects the changing composition of party coalitions, which politicians must accommodate.

This is a more speculative inference, but the declining predictive power of legislators' personal characteristics also suggests that they may not always be voting their convictions on environmental issues. The true beliefs of politicians are never fully knowable, but our best estimate of what an individual believes is what those most similar to him in sociological terms believe. If characteristics like age and education that remain associated with voters' environmental views now are much less correlated with MCs votes, perhaps it is simply because ideological purists are more likely to seek office than their moderate copartisans (Thomsen 2017). Yet ordinary voters are not subject to the same political pressures as MCs. Accordingly, the gap between voters and MCs may also reflect the latter trimming their sails for political reasons. This is significant because it suggests some would be open to changing their positions were they to perceive more political leeway.

Surveys show that party identification and environmental attitudes have become more closely associated over time. This trend may stem in part from voters taking cues from their party's leading officials, a phenomenon recently observed on environmental issues (Egan and Mullin 2017, Stokes and Warshaw 2017), much as it was earlier on other questions (Zaller 1992, Lenz 2012). Yet the resulting attitudes may also have an effect on less prominent politicians. Individual MCs cannot expect to reshape their constituents' views and must take them into account. Thus, growing mass-level party division on the environment helps explain polarization in Congress on the issue.

5.9 The Growing Partisan Divide on the Environment in the States

While the focus of this Element is national politics, examining state-level developments is useful for multiple reasons. States retain important powers in the American federal system, and their environmental policy decisions have major consequences. A study focused exclusively on national institutions also would fall short in understanding the politics of environmentalism. Environmentalists have increasingly turned to state-level initiatives given "gridlock" in Washington (Klyza and Sousa 2013). Their efforts have produced mixed results, as there is considerable variation in policy across states (Stokes and Warshaw 2017). Given the partisan divide on the environment, unified party control of state government yields very different policy outcomes in Democratic- and Republican-controlled states (Grumbach 2018).

One question I investigate is whether the parties' polarization on the environment stemmed from the regional realignment evident as the Democrats increasingly became a coastal and metropolitan party and the Republicans a Southern and rural one (Hopkins 2017, Ogarzalek 2018). To the extent we see growing party divisions on the environment within even relatively homogenous states, the claims for a chiefly geographical explanation are called into question.

Students of party position change generally have concentrated on national developments, with prominent exceptions focusing on race in the New Deal and postwar years (Chen 2009, Feinstein and Schickler 2008, Schickler 2016). Yet some issues like abortion emerged at the state level, before reaching Washington (Karol and Thurston 2014.) I first focus on developments in California, then present cross-state comparisons.

5.10 Spotlight on California

California merits special attention in a study of environmental politics. The "Golden State" has long been a leader in environmental protection; Yosemite became a state park in 1864, nearly a decade before the first national park was established at Yellowstone. More recently California's fuel efficiency and antipollution standards for cars have had a national impact, given the size of its market. It also has been the home base of environmental activism. The Sierra Club was founded in San Francisco in 1892 and is still based in the Bay Area. The Club only established chapters in other states starting in the 1950s. California was also the first state in which the Sierra Club began to endorse candidates, doing so "as an experiment" in state legislative races in 1980.[25]

California politics is also well documented. LCV scores are available for California going further back than in any other state. Figure 13 shows the growing gap between the parties on the environment in California by depicting the difference of party mean LCV ratings from 1973 to 2016.

The figure reveals that partisan divisions on environmental issues in California had grown enormously by the mid-1990s and that in this, as in so many cases, developments there foreshadowed those in the rest of the country.

Exploring state-level developments by looking at aggregate state-level data such as the difference between the average LCV ratings of party caucuses is useful, but looking more closely can further illuminate developments. The regional realignment of parties, after all, has happened not only across but also within states, as Democrats became an increasingly urban party and

---

[25] Sierra Club Board of Directors Minutes, May 3–4, 1980, pp. 21–22.

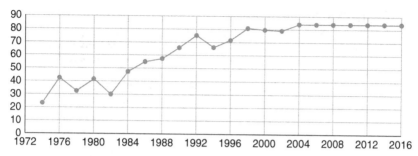

Figure 13 Difference of party mean, League of Conservation Voter Ratings, California State Assembly: 1974–2016

Republicans a more rural one. Looking at voting patterns in the California State Assembly can help assess the importance of regional shifts in producing party position change on the environment. The geographical bases of the parties *have* shifted in California, with the Democrats losing ground in their one-time stronghold, the rural central valley, while making inroads in coastal urban areas, especially in the southern part of the state. These developments received much attention when Hillary Clinton was the first Democratic Presidential nominee to carry Orange County since 1936 and when Democrats captured all of that county's congressional districts two years later,[26] but these results were only the culmination of a trend long underway (Kousser 2009).

Figure 14 reports beta coefficients from a series of ordinary least squares regressions for each legislative term in the California State Assembly from 1973 through 2000. In addition to party, the models include indicator variables reflecting whether or the legislators' districts were primarily based in northern or coastal counties, as well as a measure of the share of district residents living in urban areas.

The figure reveals that the correlation between party affiliation and LCV rating among California State Assembly members grew much stronger from the 1970s through the 1990s, even controlling for the location of their districts. This finding suggests that the geographical realignment of the parties is not the chief driver of their growing divisions on environmental policy. The same pattern – a growing partisan divide controlling for constituency factors – is evident in both Congress and the California State Assembly.

Yet while California's distinctive properties merit special attention, we cannot confidently speak about state-level developments without a wider-ranging investigation. In Table 6 I report the difference in party mean support for environmentalism for the lower house in seventeen states

---

[26] "Democrats Complete Sweep of Orange County, Once a GOP Haven," *Roll Call*, November 17, 2018.

Red, Green, and Blue

Table 6 Difference of party mean ratings on environmental
issues in state legislatures compared with Congress

	Earliest Ratings	Recent Ratings
US House	(1969–1970) 23.3	(2015–2016) 88.3
California	(1973–1974) 23.3	(2015–2016) 84
Colorado	(1997–1998) 57.5	(2015–2016) 73.9
Connecticut	(1999–2000) 9.5	(2015–2016) 14.2
Illinois	(1975–1976) 10.5	(2015–2016) 14.7
Maine	(1985–1986) 46	(2015–2016) 60.1
Maryland	(1975–1978) 7.2	(2015–2017) 66
Michigan	(2001–2002) 40.1	(2015–2016) 55
Montana	(2001–2002) 80.3	(2015–2016) 86.9
New Mexico	(2005–2006) 49.8	(2015–2016) 72.3
New York	(2003–2004) 6	(2015–2016) 29.5
North Carolina	(1999–2000) 29.1	(2015–2016) 69.3
Oregon	(1981–1982) 32.1	(2015–2016) 71.4
Texas	(1999–2000) 34.7	(2015–2016) 37.3
Utah	(1995–1996) 22.6	(2015–2016) 48.5
Virginia	(2000–2001) 24	(2016–2017) 56.4
Washington	(1989–1990) 48.4	(2015–2016) 75.7
Wisconsin	(2001–2002) 29.7	(2015–2016) 86.8

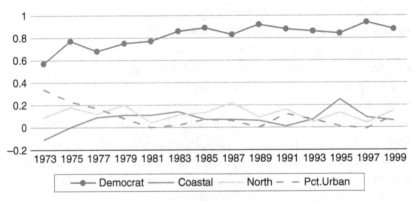

Figure 14 Predictors of support for environmentalism, California State
Assembly: 1973–2000

along with the US House as a reference point. The states are those for
which ratings of legislators are available for more than a decade, long
enough to see meaningful change. In all but two states the ratings are
from the state branch of the League of Conservation Voters. In Utah,

unusually, the Sierra Club ratings extend much further back in time, so I use them. Similarly, in New York State the organization Environmental Advocates, an affiliate of the National Wildlife Foundation, has rated state legislators since 2004, while the LCV has done so only since 2017, so I use the former group's ratings.

In most states there are no environmental ratings of state legislators or they only cover the last few years. Still, there is much diversity in terms of region and party strength in the seventeen states included in the table. The statistics also differ by state in terms of starting point. For some states, like California, Illinois, and Maryland, ratings extend back to the mid-1970s. For others, like New Mexico, they are only available since the middle of the 2000s. For all states I report the earliest ratings and those for recent years.

The statistics reported in the table reveal several things. First, in every state Democratic legislators have been more supportive than Republicans of policies favored by environmentalists since ratings were first calculated. Secondly, the partisan divide has grown everywhere. Some other notable points emerge. State legislatures generally are less polarized than Congress on environmental issues. This requires some explanation. Traditionally, state legislatures were less partisan than Congress, and this is still true of most of them (Shor 2015). Yet the gap between the states and Congress is not consistent. Some states, like California and Wisconsin, are about as polarized as Congress on the environment. Yet others, including Connecticut and Illinois, are less divided along partisan lines on the environment than the Congress of the 1970s, let alone the current one. Most states fall somewhere in between these extremes.

Why is there so much variation among states? A couple of explanations suggest themselves. One factor linked to variation in party divisions across states is political culture. Hinchliffe and Lee (2016) build on Mayhew's (1986) study of party cultures and show that states whose political culture is marked by "traditional party organizations" with an orientation toward patronage and machine politics rather than ideological activism have less polarized legislatures generally. Indeed, the correlation between Mayhew's Traditional Party Organizational scale and the interparty difference of means in recent environmental ratings for the states listed in the table is a very strong one.[27]

Another factor is the nature of party constituencies. Most states are less diverse than the country as a whole. Groups associated with opposition to environmentalism such as farmers or fossil fuel producers vary greatly in strength across states. Similarly, the highly educated voters who are the core

---

[27] Given that Mayhew calculated these state ratings in the early 1970s based on data from earlier years, their strong predictive power nearly half a century later demonstrates impressive continuity in state political culture.

of support for environmentalism are not distributed evenly throughout the country. We would expect then that in states that are economically dependent on resource extraction, legislators of both parties would be sympathetic to the demands of fossil fuel producers or agriculture. Conversely, where such economic interests are not strong and there are many highly educated voters, even Republican elected officials might see a benefit in showing a measure of sensitivity to environmental concerns.

6 How Environmentalism Has Changed

Quantitative studies of position taking on environmental issues in Congress and state legislatures as well as longitudinal studies of public opinion may suggest that "environmentalism" is a constant. Yet this is an oversimplification, if a sometimes necessary one. A study exploring the changing relationship of environmentalism and party politics must include recognition that these two phenomena are not unchanging. While the Democrats and Republicans have existed since the nineteenth century, the parties have changed in many ways. An MC who consistently voted with her party over several decades would end up changing positions on many policy questions (Karol 2009). Parties' organization has also changed greatly since the nineteenth century.

To a lesser degree this is also true of the environmental movement. The most basic fact to note is that fifty years ago even the term "environmentalism" was not prevalent. Rather, people spoke of "conservationism." This legacy is still evident in the name of the League of Conservation Voters, a leading environmentalist organization.

Is this just a question of nomenclature? Not quite. The "conservationist" ethic so prominent in the late Progressive Era overlapped only partially with what is now understood as environmentalism. Recognition of the need to protect natural resources from overuse and concern for the public interest being damaged by private firms links the two views. Yet conservationists also focused on efficiency (Hays 1959) and were far less likely to question the goal of economic growth than environmentalists in later generations. In this perspective nature was viewed in a utilitarian way as a collection of "resources" for human material benefit, even if the protection of scenic areas was deemed important and a significant role for the federal government was seen as necessary.

The more mystical view that nature should be valued independent of economic considerations and that humans are ennobled simply by being in its presence is associated with Sierra Club founder John Muir and came to be known as "preservationism." Muir had a falling out with Gifford Pinchot, the leading conservationist and a progressive Republican politician, over harvesting and replanting of trees in forests at a level that would allow the forest to survive. From Pinchot's conservationist standpoint this was wise resource use, but Muir rejected it (Meyer 1997). However, over time references to conservation came to reflect both perspectives, while the term "preservationist" was increasingly used to denote interest in protecting buildings of historical value.[28]

In recent years there has been greater recognition that many early conservationist leaders often had racist, eugenicist views. In some cases, such as Muir, they may have simply shared the "casual racism" prevalent in their era.[29]

Yet others, especially more science-minded conservationists, integrated eugenics into their world view, viewing the superior white race as something to be conserved by planning. Wohlforth (2010, 174) asserts, "[E]ugenic ideas slid frictionlessly into Pinchot's worldview, a rigidly moralistic construct of conservation, efficiency, and merit." Joseph LeConte, a Berkeley professor and John Muir's successor as President of the Sierra Club, was the scion of a plantation-owning Georgia family. In 1892 LeConte wrote, "[R]ace repulsion and race antagonism is not a wholly irrational sentiment. It is an instinct necessary for the preservation of the purity of the blood of the higher race."[30] Madison Grant, president of the New York Zoological Society, founder of the Bronx Zoo, and a leader in the campaigns to preserve the American bison and the California redwood, was also the author of the eugenicist book *The Passing of the Great Race*. Grant sought to conserve the "Nordic" race, much as he sought to conserve flora and fauna. This book was blurbed by Grant's friend Theodore Roosevelt (Spiro 2008). Grant was a member of the Boone and Crockett Club that Roosevelt founded, an elite big game hunting society that undertook some of the earliest conservation efforts.

The point is not that these figures were necessarily more racist than their political opponents. Roosevelt, Pinchot, and Grant were Republicans in an era when Democrats were staunch defenders of Jim Crow. Yet ideologies change and it is unwise to infer total continuity of ideas from a political label's use over a long period of time.[31]

Early conservationist leaders' racist, eugenicist views are not shared by today's Green activists. Yet the environmental movement long remained

---

[28] Meyer (1997) notes that the contrast between the two men should not be overdrawn. Pinchot's private writings reveal appreciation of the wonders of nature, although this was not really incorporated in his public philosophy. For his part Muir fell short of today's concept of "deep ecology" in that he valued nature for its ennobling aspect and, while recognizing the need to harvest timber, simply wanted to protect especially beautiful areas.

[29] Jedediah Purdy, "Environmentalism's Racist History," *The New Yorker*, August 13, 2015.

[30] www.sierraclub.org/yosemite-heritage-center/dr-joseph-leconte

[31] Indeed some of these leaders' views evolved as well. While Grant's views merely hardened, Wohlforth (2010, 187) argues that later in life Pinchot moved away from racist ideas. It is not clear that he ever fully shared the antisemitism and full-blown "Nordic" ideology of Grant either.

overwhelmingly white and well-to-do. Well into the mid-twentieth century some Sierra Club chapters – which organized outings and were social outlets for their members – de facto excluded nonwhites and Jews through policies requiring those seeking to join the club to be sponsored by two members. Sierra Club Executive Director David Brower's efforts to diversify the membership in the late 1950s faced resistance at a time when environmental organizations remained largely "a WASP preserve" (Fox 1981). As recently as 1990, the staffs of leading environmental groups were virtually all white.

However, in recent decades "environmental justice" has become a focus, and two people of color have served as president of the Sierra Club.[32] The growing alignment of environmentalists with the Democratic Party in an era when that party had taken on a commitment to racial equality has encouraged these developments.

Another important change concerns the name of the movement. The term "conservationism," which arose during the Progressive Era, has been largely replaced by "environmentalism." Since a change in labels often reflects some meaningful development, it is worth learning when this shift occurred. In Figure 15 I chart uses of the terms "conservationists" and "environmentalists" in two leading newspapers, the *New York Times* and *Washington Post*, from 1960 to 2017. I use these terms denoting people rather than related words like environment, environmental, or conservation because these are more likely to be used to refer to concepts unrelated to the natural world.

The figure tells a dramatic story. As the 1960s began the term "conservationists" was in use in leading papers, while "environmentalists" was not. Over the course of the 1960s the number of references to conservationists increased for several years, while "environmentalists" was still virtually unused. In the late 1960s and early 1970s, however, a remarkable shift occurred. The use of "environmentalists" skyrocketed. This is the period when the first Earth Day occurred and the EPA was created. For a few years usage of both terms grew, but eventually "conservationists" was used less, even as mentions of "environmentalists" continued to increase. To this day the latter term is used far more often in both newspapers, albeit with year-to-year fluctuation.

"Conservationists" are still mentioned more than four decades later. Yet while the absolute number of mentions of this group has actually grown in recent years, the label is used in a narrower way than it once was. A review of articles mentioning "conservationists" in both papers reveals that the term is now reserved for discussions of activism around endangered species.

---

[32] http://vault.sierraclub.org/history/presidents/default.aspx

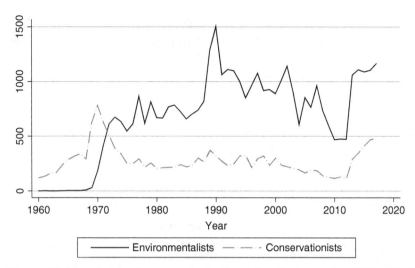

Figure 15 Use of terms "conservationists" and "environmentalists," *New York Times* and *Washington Post*: 1960–2017

By contrast, before the 1970s opposition to dam or highway construction was more apt to be described as conservationist, even when it was not chiefly based on concerns about protecting rare animals. Similarly, in the *New York Times* in 1970, 205 articles included references to both "pollution" and "conservationists," while only six did in 2000.

6.1 A Look at the Politics of Nuclear Power

During the mid-twentieth century some concerns that later became associated with environmentalism were not part of the conservationist agenda. Nuclear power is perhaps the most prominent example. Conservationist groups did not initially oppose atomic energy. As Gamson and Modigliani (1989, 15) note, from the 1950s through the mid-1960s "there was no significant anti nuclear-power discourse . . . Nuclear power was, in general, a non-issue."

While some grass roots activists had already become suspicious of nuclear power generally, much of the rhetoric in the earliest local controversies was focused on the desire to protect certain scenic locations or on claims that they were unsafe sites for power plants. Both concerns were invoked in Bodega Bay, California, the first case in which activists blocked the construction of a plant. This 1964 victory for antinuclear activists relied on not only worries about damage to scenery but safety concerns based on the proximity of the proposed plant site to the San Andreas Fault.[33]

---

[33] "P. G. & E. Gives Up on Atom Plant at Bodega Bay," *Los Angeles Times*, October 31, 1964, p. 8.

The Sierra Club initially viewed nuclear power as a source of "clean energy," and their opposition to the proposed Bodega plant was based solely on "aesthetics and wilderness preservation" (Wellock 1992, 196). In internal debates, Club leaders rejected raising safety concerns that might call use of nuclear power more generally into question (Wellock 1992, 201–202). Safety concerns, however, were raised by a grassroots group called The Association to Preserve Bodega Head. This organization cited not only the proximity to the fault line, but also alleged dangers to local dairy production, based on findings that atmospheric nuclear testing had contaminated food.[34]

Environmentalists' attitudes toward nuclear power changed in the late 1960s and early 1970s. David Brower, the long-time Executive Director of the Sierra Club, was ousted in 1969. Many issues were involved, but one factor was his turn against nuclear power, which other Club leaders were not ready to follow (Turner 2015). Brower's new group, The Friends of the Earth, took an antinuclear stand from its inception in 1969.

However, even with Brower gone the Sierra Club gradually turned against nuclear power. In 1972 the Club's Board of Directors voted to remain neutral on a California ballot measure backed by Ralph Nader that would – among other things – institute a five-year moratorium on nuclear plant construction. It also rejected a proposal to oppose research on the liquid fast metal breeder reactor (Schrepfer 1992, 231).

Yet that same year the Club called for a revision of the Price-Anderson law, a federal statute that limited the liability of utilities that operated nuclear plants and provided public insurance.[35] Changes in this law – which still exists – could have discouraged firms from building new plants or even led them to decommission existing ones since the risk of vast claims following a nuclear accident made it difficult for utilities to purchase adequate insurance in the private market. By the end of 1972 the Sierra Club was sufficiently suspicious of nuclear power to endorse a joint statement with the antinuclear Friends of the Earth, the League of Conservation Voters, and other groups "expressing concern about an impending huge increase in nuclear power production in coming years."[36]

In early 1974 the Sierra Club went further, calling unambiguously for a moratorium on the construction of new nuclear power plants. The Wilderness Society followed suit (Schrepfer 1992, 233). Finally, after the

---

[34] David Pesonen, a young Sierra Club staffer, was actually a leading organizer of this group, but he did not represent the Club in doing so.

[35] www.sierraclub.org/policy/energy/nuclear-power

[36] "Ecology Conscious Wanted on Congress Atomic Body," *Independent Press Telegram* (Long Beach), December 31, 1972, p. 10.

1979 Three Mile Island incident, the Club called for the "phased closure and decommissioning "of existing nuclear plants."[37]

The Democratic Party generally lagged environmentalists on nuclear power. In their 1964 platform Democrats bragged about the growth of atomic energy on their watch, noting, "The number of civilian nuclear power plants has increased from 3 to 14 since January 1961; and now the advent of economic nuclear power provides utilities a wider choice of competitive power sources in many sections of the country."[38] The 1968 Democratic platform called for "development of 'breeder' reactors and large-scale nuclear desalting plants" as well as international cooperation in "the non-military use of atomic energy." The 1972 Democratic platform, written by supporters of George McGovern, betrayed no concern about nuclear power.

Only in 1976, two years after Sierra Club had called for a moratorium on nuclear plant construction, and six years after the creation of the antinuclear Friends of the Earth and League of Conservation Voters, did Democrats modify their position, asserting, "U.S. dependence on nuclear power should be kept to the minimum necessary to meet our needs. We should apply stronger safety standards as we regulate its use. And we must be honest with our people concerning its problems and dangers as well as its benefits."[39] This chronology suggests that politicians were not leading interest groups, but rather following them.

Figure 16 illustrates the antinuclear trend among environmentalists. The figure charts mentions of nuclear power in *New York Times* or *Washington Post* articles that also include the word "conservationists" or "environmentalists." (I use both terms because the antinuclear movement arose when "conservationist" was still the more frequent descriptor.) From 1960 through 1962 there were no such articles. The first articles linking these terms appeared in 1963 and 1964, and generally did not suggest that these groups were opposed to nuclear power in principle but rather that they had concerns about certain proposed plant locations. However, as antinuclear sentiment increased, chiefly in the early 1970s, articles mentioning environmentalists or conservationists and nuclear power became far more common and it was clear that they were opposed to use of this technology in general.

The figure reveals that the mentions of environmentalists/conservationists in connection with nuclear power declined after the early 1980s, although they did not disappear. This decline reflects the declining salience of the topic in political debates as utility companies stopped commissioning new plants after the 1979

---

[37] Ibid.   [38] "Political Party Platforms," The American Presidency Project, www.ucsb.edu.
[39] Ibid.

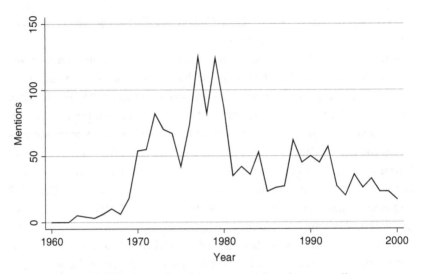

Figure 16 Mentions of nuclear power and environmentalists or conservationists, *New York Times* and *Washington Post*: 1960–2000

Three Mile Island incident. While construction on some plants not yet completed in 1979 continued, the Nuclear Regulatory Commission did not approve any new ones until 2012.[40]

Given increasing concerns about climate change, some environmentalists have argued that nuclear power is a lesser evil than fossil fuels. For many years journalists have been suggesting that climate change has changed minds about nuclear power.[41] If so, this would be a return to much older attitudes. Leading conservationists, including David Brower, once argued that nuclear power was preferable to some enormous hydropower projects and coal-burning plants (Schrepfer 1992, 229, Turner 2015, 188). Yet this has *not* become the mainstream position among environmental organizations, which still prefer to focus on conservation and renewables like solar and wind power.

The fact that what it means to be an environmentalist has changed in policy terms is hardly unique. In many policy areas debates evolve. In the 1930s support for antilynching legislation and opposition to the poll tax was enough to put one on the antiracist side. By the 1970s measures that once were unimaginable such as busing to achieve school integration and affirmative action became prominent parts of the civil rights agenda.

---

[40] NRC Approves First New Nuclear Plant in a Generation," *Reuters.com*, February 9, 2012.
[41] "Climate Bill Could Turn Friends into Foes as Some Go Nuclear," *Los Angeles Times* April 9, 2007, p. 1; "Nuclear Power Finding Favor in Unusual Place," *Baltimore Sun*, May 16, 2005, p. 4a; "Nuclear Power Advocated to Slow Warming," *St. Louis Post Dispatch*, November 4, 2013, p. 9; "Interest in Nuclear Power Sparked in Calif.," *Chicago Tribune*, December 10, 2015, p. 18.

7 Environmentalism and the Politics of Party Coalitions

The integration of environmental organizations in the Democratic Party is a major development. It is part of a broader trend toward polarization in which other "single-issue" groups have been drawn into one party or the other. For example, like environmentalists, the National Rifle Association did not support presidential candidates prior to the 1980s.

Interest groups have traditionally made a show of bipartisanship. This is true for multiple reasons. They seek to avoid being taken for granted by the party with which they are de facto aligned. They hope to encourage elected officials from the less friendly party to break from the ranks at least sometimes. They also wish to have credibility in the media. Yet in an era of polarization, this posture is increasingly difficult to sustain.

These tensions were on display in the case of the 2006 Rhode Island US Senate race. Incumbent Republican Senator Lincoln Chafee was facing a tough fight for reelection in a Democratic state at a time when President Bush was unpopular. Chafee, who generally received high marks from environmental groups, won endorsements from the LCV and Sierra Club as well as other lobbies that usually supported Democrats including NARAL.

Some Democratic activists criticized the environmental organizations and other progressive "single-issue groups" that backed Chafee. Markos Moulitsas, the founder of the activist website dailykos.com, found fault with some of Chafee's positions, but his chief argument was that the concerns of environmentalists and other Democratic-leaning progressive constituencies would be best served if Democrats regained control of the Senate. Chafee, for all of his Green votes, ultimately would empower other Republicans who would use their majority status in the Senate in ways inimical to the concerns of environmentalists, Moulitsas contended.[42] In the end Chafee was defeated by Democrat Sheldon Whitehouse and later left the GOP, winning a gubernatorial race in Rhode Island as an independent in 2010, and later mounting a brief bid for the 2016 Democratic presidential nomination.

A change in tax law in 1975 made it possible for the Sierra Club and other nonprofit organizations to take a more visible role in politics, even to the extent of endorsing candidates. However, the Club proceeded cautiously. In February 1976, after months of discussion, the environmental lobby created a political arm, the Sierra Club Committee on Political Education (SCCOPE).

Yet the Club still proceeded very cautiously. In the spring of 1976 the requests by two candidates for the Democratic presidential nomination, former Georgia Governor Jimmy Carter and US Representative Morris Udall of Arizona,

---

[42] "RI Sen: Morons at the Sierra Club," www.dailykos.com/stories/2006/4/19/203557/-

provoked a debate within the organization. The candidates sought access to the Club's mailing list. The Club board debated whether to give candidates access for purposes of sending campaign material to members, but not fundraising appeals. While eight of 14 board members agreed, they lacked the two-thirds vote needed and the Club rejected the candidates' request.[43] This is especially striking because Carter was by then the likely Democratic nominee and Udall was a long-time supporter of environmental causes and in line to become Chairman of the House Interior Committee, which had jurisdiction over public lands.[44]

In late 1976 the Sierra Club Bulletin included an extended comparison of the environmental records of President Gerald Ford and the Democratic presidential nominee, Jimmy Carter.[45] Hundreds of thousands of copies were printed and distributed. The contrast was clearly favorable to Carter, but there was no official endorsement.[46] Similarly, in 1976, the League of Conservation Voters, which had previously focused on Congressional races, described Jimmy Carter, then the Democratic presidential nominee, as "outstanding" and President Gerald Ford as "hopeless." Yet the group stopped short of a formal endorsement that year.[47] Unlike the LCV, which had been active in Congressional races since 1970, the Club did not endorse candidates in the 1978 midterm election.

In 1980 the Sierra Club edged closer to partisan politics. It allowed the presidential candidates "courting the environmental community" access to the mailing list. However, these candidates included not only the aspirants for the Democratic nomination, President Carter, Senator Ted Kennedy, and California Governor Jerry Brown, but also two Republican contenders, US Representative John Anderson of Illinois and former CIA Director George H. W. Bush.[48]

Anderson was not long for the GOP, failing to win a single primary. He later ran as a third-party candidate in 1980. Bush, however, won the Iowa Caucus and six primaries, emerging as Ronald Reagan's strongest rival for the Republican nomination. This showing led to Bush's selection as Reagan's running mate once negotiations with Gerald Ford failed. Bush was not a Sierra Club favorite as Vice President or President and he discarded other stands during the Reagan years – he had been pro-choice and once dismissed supply-side tax policy as

---

[43] Sierra Club Board of Directors Minutes (Online Archive of California), May 1–2, 1976, pp. 28–31.

[44] "Environmental Leader Mo Udall Dies," *Washington Post*, December 14, 1998, p. E6.

[45] "National Sierra Club Breaking with Tradition This Campaign," *Cincinnati Enquirer*, October 25, 1976, p. 28.

[46] The national League of Conservation Voters was also formally neutral in 1976, but the California chapter supported Carter. "Seven Senators Given Perfect Vote Scorecards,"*The Sun-Telegram* (San Bernardino), October 22, 1976, p. 5.

[47] "Conservationists Give Carter High Marks and Ford Low Ones," *New York Times*, August 22, 1976.

[48] Sierra Club Board of Directors Minutes, February 2–3, 1980, pp. 26–27.

"voodoo economics" (Karol 2009). Still, it is notable that as late as 1980 serious Republican presidential candidates thought it worthwhile to court Sierra Club members, and Club leaders were happy to help them.

In the fall of 1980 the Club took another step toward open alignment with Democrats by allowing its leading officials, including Club President Joe Fontaine and Executive Director Carl Pope, to publicly support President Carter, albeit in their personal capacities.[49] In a meeting at the White House, environmental leaders, including Sierra Club officials, publicly supported President Carter on a personal basis.

In later years the Club gradually abandoned its historic policy of political neutrality. In 1982 the Sierra Club began to endorse congressional candidates. The first endorsee was Rep. Sidney Yates, a liberal Democrat who chaired the House Appropriations Subcommittee on the Interior. In an October 1982 report, SCCOPE listed Congressional candidates it had endorsed. Only six of 90 were Republicans, all of them incumbents.[50]

The inexorable logic of the American two-party system drew the Club into the Democratic Party during Reagan's first term. The Club agreed without internal controversy to give aspirants for the Democratic presidential nomination access to their mailing list.[51] In November 1983 the Club went on the record against a prospective independent bid for the presidency by former US Representative John Anderson, who had taken many stands the Club approved of in his failed 1980 presidential campaign. While commending Anderson's record, the Club resolved it did not "believe that an independent Anderson campaign will effectively serve our common environmental objectives."[52]

By 1984 it was clear the Sierra Club would oppose Reagan. Having been unwilling to formally endorse Carter in 1980, they took the remarkable step of publicly opposing Reagan's reelection in February 1984, long before it was even clear who his Democratic opponent would be. The Club termed the Reagan administration "the worst of all time" and resolved that he "must be defeated." This was followed by a pro forma call for "the announcement of Republican challengers with good environmental records," although it was evident that Reagan would be renominated without opposition.[53] In the fall of

---

[49] Sierra Club Minutes, September 6–7, 1980, p. 16.
[50] Sierra Club Committee on Political Education Memo, August 20, 1982; Sierra Club Board of Directors Minutes, September 11–12, 1982.
[51] Jesse Jackson and George McGovern's campaigns both sought and received access to the Club mailing list. For McGovern, see Sierra Club Minutes, November 19–20, 1983, p. 21. For Jackson, see Sierra Club Minutes, February 4–5, 1984, pp. 17–18.
[52] Sierra Club Minutes, November 19–20, 1983, p. 22.
[53] Sierra Club Minutes, February 4–5, 1984, p. 22.

1984 the Sierra Club formally endorsed a presidential candidate for the first time in its 92-year history when it rallied to the side of Walter Mondale, Reagan's Democratic opponent.[54] The League of Conservation Voters likewise backed the former Vice President.[55]

The Sierra Club was more cautious during the 1988 presidential campaign than they had been in 1984. This time they did not endorse the Democratic nominee, Massachusetts governor Michael Dukakis.[56] The Club leaders did not even "personally" back Dukakis, as they had Jimmy Carter in 1980. What explains this retreat?

George H. W. Bush did send different signals from Ronald Reagan. In 1980 Bush had sought access to the Club mailing list when seeking the Republican presidential nomination. In 1988 the Vice President pledged to be "the environmental president" and spoke about some environmental issues in his 1988 acceptance speech as part of his call for a "kinder, gentler nation." Bush even mounted an attack on Dukakis for the polluted state of Boston Harbor.[57] After the election SCCOPE Chair Carl Pope told the Sierra Club Board that "[t]he Presidential race was different this year for the Sierra Club because each candidate was courting the environmental vote."[58]

Yet Club leaders do not seem to have thought Dukakis and Bush were truly equivalent. Before the election Pope said, "Michael Dukakis gives environmental issues a great deal of weight. They're not the most important thing to him, but they're up there. George Bush thinks environmental protection is a nice thing and he's willing to have government do it, but it's way down his priority list."[59]

Nor is it plausible that Mondale's overwhelming defeat four years earlier was sufficient to deter the Club from stepping once more into the breach. To be sure, interest groups often seek to endorse likely winners and shun hopeless candidates in order to make their endorsement seem valuable. Yet, unlike Mondale, Dukakis was actually leading in the polls during the summer of the

---

[54] "Sierra Club Breaks Its Tradition and Backs a Candidate: Mondale," *New York Times*, September 20, 1984.

[55] "Mondale Picks up Support," *Evening Sun* (Baltimore), August 29, 1984, p. 3.

[56] "Environmentalists Call Bush's Campaign Claims. 'Hypocrisy,'" *Austin American-Statesman*, October 26, 1988, p. 29.

[57] "Address Accepting the Presidential Nomination at the Republican National Convention in New Orleans," August 18, 1988, archived at The American Presidency Project, www.presidency .ucsb.edu; "Boston Harbor Cleanup Puts Dukakis on the Spot," *Washington Post*, August 11, 1988.

[58] Sierra Club Minutes, November 19–20, 1988, p. 38.

[59] "Candidates Promise Environmental Amends," *Wisconsin State Journal*, September 18, 1988, p. 41.

election year.[60] In the end the Massachusetts governor ran only slightly better than Mondale had, carrying just ten states and the District of Columbia. Yet he had been expected to much fare better, making it unlikely that the Sierra Club's failure to embrace him was based chiefly on a view that he was doomed.

Instead, lingering concerns about appearing to be in one partisan camp seem to have influenced Club leaders. An interest group may endorse candidates for lesser office, but as long as some nominees from each party are backed, a pretense of nonpartisanship may be maintained, even if the division is far from 50–50. However, the presidency is indivisible. Presidential endorsements are far better publicized than others and can be more of a defining choice for an interest group.

After the 1984 election, Club leaders worried that people had misinterpreted their unprecedented endorsement of Walter Mondale. Sierra Club Committee on Political Education (SCCOPE) Chair Richard Fiddler told the Board of Directors, "It is important for the Club to emphasize that it is a bi-partisan organization and is willing to go the extra mile to maintain that status. Endorsement of Mondale was incorrectly viewed by many as endorsement of the Democratic Party."[61]

In our far more polarized era the Sierra Club leaders' concerns about seeming partisan may seem quaint. Indeed, 1988 was the last time the Sierra Club failed to endorse the Democratic Presidential nominee. Even at the time other leading environmental groups did not share the Sierra Club's reticence. The League of Conservation Voters and the Friends of the Earth, both founded by David Brower who had been forced out of the Sierra Club Executive Directorship in part for excessive militancy, endorsed Dukakis.[62]

One way to understand the trend in environmentalists' interaction with the parties is to move beyond a focus on presidential races and look at endorsements of congressional candidates. The LCV has endorsed candidates since its founding in 1970, more than a decade before the Sierra Club began doing so, although even they stayed out of presidential elections in the 1970s. While the LCV supported Dukakis (unlike the Sierra Club), its pattern of campaign contributions showed greater openness to Republicans than those of the older environmental lobby (Dominguez and Skinner 2014). Endorsements from 1970 to the

---

[60] "Poll Shows Dukakis Leads Bush: Many Reagan Backers Switch Sides," *New York Times*, May 17, 1988, p. A1; "Dukakis Lead Widens According to New Poll," *New York Times*, July 26, 1988, p. A17.
[61] "SCCOPE Report," Sierra Club Board of Directors Minutes, December 1–2, 1984, p. 2.
[62] "Nature Coalition to Endorse Dukakis," *Star Tribune* (Minneapolis), September 15, 1988, p. 9. Interestingly, however, Dominguez and Skinner (2014) found that from the 1980s through the 2000s the LCV gave a greater share of its campaign contributions to Republicans than the Sierra Club did.

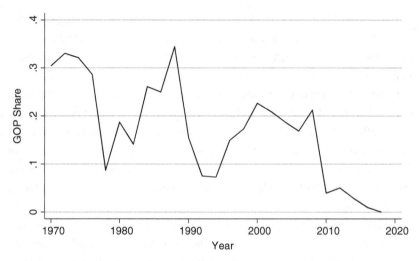

Figure 17 Republican share of LCV endorsements, congressional races: 1970–2018

present are shown in Figure 17. Endorsements from 1990 through 2018 were provided by the LCV. I compiled endorsements for earlier years by using news stories archived in the Newspapers.com database.[63] They reveal that while a majority of the LCV's endorsements went to Democratic candidates from the group's inception, for many years a significant minority of endorsees were Republicans. There are short-term oscillations, but a clear downward trend is evident.

7.1 How Party Coalition Dynamics Have Influenced Environmental Organizations

When interest groups become aligned with parties, they end up sharing space with other factions with different concerns. Over time presence in a party coalition can reorient a group in important ways. This may be due to strategic calculation in which groups decide to "log-roll," i.e., actively support each other's policies and not just back the same candidates. It may also result from conviction, as a group's activist members and leadership are resocialized ideologically.

One example of this dynamic is the issue of immigration. Since the 1960s the Sierra Club had been on record seeking to stabilize or reduce the US population. In 1978 the Club called for a congressional "review" of immigration policies that would assess their possible impact on population trends, the "disproportionate

---

[63] News stories were found via search of election years using key words "League of Conservation Voters" and "endors*". In some cases in early years endorsements were announced by state chapters of LCV, which generally focus on state-level elections.

burden on certain states," and "the effect of immigration on population growth and environmental quality in this country" (Clarke 2001, 20). The wording of this resolution suggested that the Club did not share Emma Lazarus's views of immigration, but they did not focus on restriction in the years to come.

In the 1990s and 2000s, however, there was a grassroots anti-immigration campaign within the Sierra Club.[64] There were two key junctures in this failed movement. In 1998 there was a referendum of the Club's membership in which 60 percent voted to retain a neutral policy. In ensuing years, however, some immigration restrictionists were elected to the Board of Directors. In 2004 a slate of anti-immigration candidates led by former Colorado Governor Richard Lamm, a Democrat, ran for seats on the Board. The election of this slate would have given restrictionists a majority, but it was overwhelmingly defeated. Turnout was much higher than in the 1998 referendum. The Club held another vote in 2005, and the antirestrictionist forces won by a greater than five-to-one margin.[65] The Club still formally embraced the goal of stabilizing the US population, but only by dealing with "root causes" of migration.

King (2008) argues that many Sierra Club members who opposed the restrictionist campaign did not oppose limits on immigration in principle. She found that those dedicated to antiracist "environmental justice" activism who categorically rejected restriction were in the minority. Instead the large pivotal group of members that doomed the restrictionist campaign feared that the adoption of such a policy would split the Club, make it appear racist, and alienate allies.

More recently the Club has taken a new tack on immigration. While insisting it was not "modifying the existing policy," it backed comprehensive immigration reform with "an equitable path to citizenship" in 2013. In 2017 the Sierra Club Board of Directors approved a resolution retroactively endorsing the DACA and DAPA policies instituted by President Obama as well as the Dream Act. The League of Conservation Voters also took a pro-Dreamer stand.[66] Environmental lobbies' traditional concern about population growth long ago led them to favor family planning and reproductive rights. They have maintained this position, which, unlike hostility to immigration, aligns them with other key elements of the Democratic Party.[67]

---

[64] The Wilderness Society did adopt such a position in 1996 and seems to have maintained it at least until 2000. See Clarke (2001) and "Earth Day Founder Warns of Population Growth," *Wisconsin State Journal*, March 30, 2000, p. 1b.

[65] "Anti-Migrant Slate Rejected by Sierra Club," *Los Angeles Times*, April 22, 2004, p. 1; "Sierra Club Members Vote to Remain Neutral in the Immigration Debate," *Los Angeles Times*, April 26, 2005, p. 87.

[66] www.sierraclub.org/policy/immigration, http://origin.lcv.org/article/lcv-calls-congress-protect-dreamers-temporary-protective-status/

[67] www.sierraclub.org/compass/2016/01/roe-v-wade-43-years-later

The entry of environmentalists into the Democratic coalition has not been without complications. Their chief intracoalitional antagonist has been organized labor. Unions in several industries including loggers, the building trades, and autoworkers have at times opposed policies supported by environmentalists. Yet these disagreements have generally been manageable (Obach 2002, 2004) and they have diminished. In some cases the unions have moved toward environmentalists' views, while in others the Green lobbies have adopted organized labor's position.

The recent case of the Keystone XL pipeline controversy illustrates the first dynamic. The changing composition of the labor movement has reduced tensions between unions and environmentalists. Organized labor has been in decline for decades, but this trend has not been equally evident across unions. The relative importance of public sector unions has increased vis-à-vis private sector ones, especially those in manufacturing and construction. This has meant that the unions most likely to be at odds with environmentalists are less and less central to decision-making within the AFL-CIO, making it easier for the labor federation to preserve good relations with environmentalists.

After much discussion, in 2013 the AFL-CIO leadership did endorse the Keystone XL Pipeline, a vast project designed to transport oil from western Canada to the Gulf of Mexico that was strongly supported by the "building trades" or construction unions. When the labor federation did so in 2013, Sierra Club President Michael Brune acknowledged that it caused "tensions" between environmentalists and unions.[68]

However, it is notable that the labor federation did not include votes on the pipeline in calculating their annual ratings of Members of Congress.[69] This meant that a legislator could stay in the good graces of the AFL-CIO – if not all its constituent unions – even if they opposed the pipeline. The declining labor movement has an interest in maintaining good relations with coalition partners like environmentalists and minimizing conflict where it is inevitable.[70] By contrast, the League of Conservation Voters did include votes on the pipeline in their ratings of legislators, showing that the issue was a higher priority for them.

This difference in intensity of concern about the pipeline expressed by the two segments of the Democratic coalition was reflected in Congressional

---

[68] "A.F.L.-C.I.O. Backs Keystone Oil Pipeline, If Indirectly," *New York Times*, February 28, 2013, p. B2.

[69] https://aflcio.org/what-unions-do/social-economic-justice/advocacy/scorecard/us-senate-score card; https://aflcio.org/what-unions-do/social-economic-justice/advocacy/scorecard/us-house-scorecard

[70] "AFL-CIO Courts Sierra Club Despite Keystone Disagreement," *Bloomberg.com*, September 9, 2013.

Democrats' behavior. Only ten Democratic senators and 29 Democratic representatives voted for Keystone in January 2015, and President Obama ultimately vetoed the bill.[71] Notably, the Democratic MCs who backed Keystone were generally *not* those closest to organized labor, but rather moderates and those from states where traditional energy production was more important economically, or where jobs would be created by the construction and operation of the proposed pipeline.

On trade policy environmentalists have moved closer to the views of labor unions. In the first postwar decades, American labor unions generally supported trade liberalization. Yet by the early 1970s the rise of imports, most notably from Japan, threatened American jobs and wage levels, and the AFL-CIO took a protectionist turn. In the 1970s and 1980s their pressures helped reverse the orientation of Congressional Democrats, who had been the relatively pro-trade caucus since the nineteenth century (Karol 2009).

Environmentalists were not initially part of this story. Trade policy was not a concern of theirs. In the 1990s, however, leading environmental groups became critical of trade agreements and began to work against "fast track" negotiating authority alongside unions (Shoch 2001). Much as unions insisted on labor standards in potential trading partners, environmentalists raised concerns about the relocation of economic activity to countries with less stringent environmental regulations. While environmentalists' focus was not identical to that of the unions, it led them in the same direction – skepticism concerning the free trade agreements long promoted by presidents of both parties. The BlueGreen Alliance, a grouping formed in 2006 by the Sierra Club and Steelworkers, now includes many other labor and environmental organizations pledged to seek "good jobs, clean infrastructure and fair trade."[72] All in all, there has been a convergence between unions and environmentalists that, while not total, has allowed both groups to coexist within the Democratic coalition.

In late 2018 a proposal called the Green New Deal (GND) received widespread attention. The GND includes calls to address climate change via massive infrastructure investment to "achieve net-zero greenhouse gas emissions" by 2030, but also includes calls for guaranteed jobs with paid leave and health care, education, housing, and retirement security for all, anti-monopoly measures, and protections for minorities and union workers. By late February 2019 the resolution had 89 House and 11 Senate co-sponsors, all Democrats except for independent Senator Bernie Sanders. Backers included several prominent

---

[71] www.senate.gov/legislative/LIS/roll_call_lists/roll_call_vote_cfm.cfm?congress=114&session=1& vote=00049; www.govtrack.us/congress/votes/114-2015/h75; "Obama Vetoes Keystone Pipeline," *Chicago Tribune,* February 25, 2015, p. 1.
[72] www.bluegreenalliance.org/about/

aspirants for the Democratic presidential nomination besides Sanders, including Senators Cory Booker, Kirsten Gillibrand, Kamala Harris, Amy Klobuchar, and Elizabeth Warren.[73]

Critics, including even Republicans with a record of environmental concern and some Democrats, charged that the GND resolution contained no support for nuclear power or a carbon tax while including provisions on unrelated issues that would repel many worried about climate change.[74] GND backers replied that most Republicans show no interest in addressing climate change, so the benefit of a proposal that addresses concerns of other elements of the Democratic coalition and moves up on the party's agenda outweighs the risk of alienating moderates and the few Republicans who might support some more narrowly focused measures to address climate change.[75]

The GND is an aspirational statement endorsed by only a minority of congressional Democrats and unlikely to result in legislation soon. Yet the resolution is the culmination of the decades-long process I describe in this Element. In it environmental concerns are linked to and arguably subsumed within a broader progressive agenda championed by one party, the Democrats.

7.2 Environmentalists and the Politics of Judicial Nominations

Another area that illustrates the growing alignment of environmentalists with other interest groups in the Democratic coalition is judicial nominations. In recent decades appointments to the federal courts have been increasingly contentious. The greatest controversy has surrounded Supreme Court nominations, which increasingly result in near party-line voting. Yet appointments to the lower federal courts – once largely uncontroversial – have also become divisive in recent decades (Binder and Maltzman 2002, Scherer 2005).

An important aspect of this conflict is the increasing role of interest groups in fights over judicial nominations. Judicial decisions affect many policy areas, so lobbies that would focus on different bills in Congress may share an interest in promoting or opposing a judicial nomination. This is not entirely new; in 1930 combined opposition from the American Federation of Labor and the National

---

[73] www.congress.gov/bill/116th-congress/house-resolution/109/text; www.congress.gov/bill/116th-congress/senate-resolution/59

[74] http://nymag.com/intelligencer/2019/02/democrats-need-a-climate-plan-the-green-new-deal-isnt-it.html; www.politico.com/magazine/story/2019/01/15/the-trouble-with-the-green-new-deal-223977; www.rollcall.com/news/opinion/time-green-true-deal-progressive-environment-climate-change

[75] www.vox.com/energy-and-environment/2019/2/23/18228142/green-new-deal-critics. Some unions remain skeptical of the Green New Deal at present, however (www.rollcall.com/news/congress/green-new-deal-democrats-fence).

Association for the Advancement of Colored People led to the defeat of Herbert Hoover's Supreme Court nominee, Judge John Parker (Watson 1963). Yet after the Parker fight there was little controversy over individual judicial nominations again until the late 1960s, when backlash to the Warren Court's role in promoting civil rights developed.

The core of the liberal alliance active in fights over judicial nominations was organized labor and African-American groups. In 1930, when these two lobbies were not generally allied, their shared opposition to Judge Parker kept him off the Supreme Court. The same groups supported the unsuccessful nomination of Abe Fortas in 1968 and helped defeat Nixon's nominees, Clement Haynsworth and Harold Carswell, in 1969 and 1970. Newly mobilized feminists also joined labor and civil rights groups in opposing Carswell (Kalman 2017).

Environmental groups were latecomers to the progressive interest group coalition focused on the courts. They were absent from the battles over the Fortas, Haynsworth, and Carswell nominations from 1968 to 1970. Starting in the 1970s, however, environmental groups increasingly saw the courts as an important arena where policy was often fleshed out. The Sierra Club Legal Defense Fund was founded in 1971 (Mitchell, Mertig and Dunlap 1991, 226). Yet even though they were increasingly active in the courts, environmentalists stayed out of the fight over the elevation of William Rehnquist from Associate to Chief Justice in 1986.

Only in 1987 with Ronald Reagan's nomination of Robert Bork did the Sierra Club and other environmental groups enter the fray to oppose the President's choice for the high court. Environmental groups noted that, as an appellate court judge, Bork had almost always ruled against allowing citizens to sue governmental agencies in environmental matters but had frequently sided with business interests against those same regulators.[76]

While the Bork confirmation fight was a milestone, it did not begin an era in which environmentalists were entrenched in the progressive coalition fighting judicial nominations. Unlike labor unions, feminists, and most civil rights groups, the Sierra Club was not active in the fight over Clarence Thomas's highly controversial nomination in 1991.[77] As in the case of their support for Mondale, the Sierra Club viewed the Bork nomination as a special case.

Yet starting in 2003, Green groups including Earthjustice (the former Sierra Club Legal Defense Fund) began to align with other progressive groups to oppose controversial judicial nominees picked by President George W. Bush. William G. Myers, a nominee to the 9th Circuit Court of Appeals, was the first

---

[76] "Bork Nomination was 'Last Straw'," *Tampa Bay Times*, October 11, 1987.
[77] "Who's against, Who's for Thomas," *Indianapolis News*, August 1, 1991, p. 2.

judicial nominee opposed by Senate Democrats largely on the basis of his environmental record.[78] In 2003 the League of Conservation Voters for the first time also included a vote on one of President Bush's nominees for an appellate court, former Alabama Attorney General William Pryor.[79]

However, despite their increasing involvement in lower court fights, environmental groups did not contest the nomination of John Roberts, first as Associate Justice and then, following the death of William Rehnquist, as Chief Justice in 2005.[80] Nor did they take a stand on the short-lived nomination of Harriet Miers. Environmental lobbies including the Sierra Club, Friends of the Earth, Earthjustice, and Greenpeace did, however, oppose the nomination of Samuel Alito later that year. This was the first time the Green lobbies had opposed a high court nominee since the Bork nomination nearly twenty years earlier.[81]

Since then environmentalists have consistently been involved in Supreme Court confirmations, endorsing President Obama's nominees, Sonia Sotomayor and Elena Kagan, and opposing President Trump's choices, Neil Gorsuch and Brett Kavanaugh.[82] Environmentalists' presence in the coalition of progressive, court-focused interest groups was institutionalized when they joined umbrella organizations active in judicial nominations. The Sierra Club is a member of the Leadership Conference for Civil and Human Rights (LCCR). Both the Sierra Club Foundation and the League of Conservation Voters Action Fund are members of the Alliance for Justice.[83]

7.3 Coalition Dynamics and Environmental Politics within the Republican Party

In this Element the relationship between environmental groups and other constituencies of the contemporary Democratic Party has received the most attention. Yet coalition dynamics in both parties are important. Were it not for Republican resistance to environmentalists' agenda, the issue would not be a partisan one.

---

[78] "Partisan Vote Advances Bush Judge Nominee," *Los Angeles Times*, April 2, 2004.

[79] "Green Gridlock," *National Review*, July 23, 2004; League of Conservation Voters, *2003 National Environmental Scorecard*, p. 18.

[80] "Enviros Back Sotomayor for Supreme Court," *Grist*, July 13, 2009; "Environmental Groups Smile on Kagan's Ascension," *Environmental News Service*, August 6, 2010; "Colorado Native, Neil Gorsuch Would Bring Distinctive Western Touch to Supreme Court," McClatchy DC Bureau, February 3, 2017; "New Trump Supreme Court Pick Gives Environmental Groups a Lot to Fear as Consensus Strategy Emerges," *ThinkProgress*, July 10, 2018.

[81] "Release All Alito Documents, Senate Democrats Insist," *Philadelphia Inquirer*, December 21, 2005, p. 13.

[82] "Sierra Club Buying Ad to Target Gorsuch Vote," *The Hill*, April 1, 2017.

[83] www.afj.org/about-afj/member-organizations

The Republican coalition has changed as well. Even though the Republican coalition included business interests before the rise of environmentalism, there have been successive waves of pro-development, pro-resource use mobilization in the GOP since the 1970s that have helped pull that party's elected officials away from support for environmental regulation. Corporate interests have funded think-tanks, conservative public interest legal foundations, and subsidized pro-development activists (Layzer 2012, Turner and Isenberg 2018).

In the late 1970s and early 1980s the Sagebrush Rebellion, located chiefly in the West and focused on restrictions on use of federal land, had an impact on the environmental policies of the Reagan administration before provoking a backlash. In the 1990s, the "wise use" movement was more widespread and somewhat more successful (Turner 2009). Groups like "People for the West!" won corporate funding but included authentic local activists (Turner and Isenberg 2018).

More recently, the most dramatic development has been the massive involvement of Charles and David Koch, heirs to a vast oil fortune, in conservative and Republican politics since the 1990s. Their political activity dates back further. Charles Koch was the chief patron of the libertarian Cato Institute that was established in 1977.[84] Until the 1994 campaign cycle, however, Koch Industries was not a leading Republican donor. In that cycle the firm was the seventh largest source of contributions in the oil and gas sector, according to Federal Election Commission data analyzed by the Center for Responsive Politics.[85]

The Koch brothers stood out even in the generally conservative and Republican-aligned oil and gas sector. From the first, their goals were more ideological and their contributions skewed more Republican. In 1994, when oil and gas donors gave 63 percent of their contributions to GOP candidates, 94.6 percent of the Koch's donations went to Republicans. They were the seventh largest donor in the sector that year, but the second largest by 1998 and the largest in 2006 and in most cycles since then. Comparing these two percentages slightly understates the early distinctiveness of the Koch brothers in that their funds are included in the sector total and without them the share of contributions from it to Republicans in 1994 would be less than 63 percent. The Kochs also were among "the leading funders of climate change denial actors and activities," especially after ExxonMobil pulled back (Dunlap and McCright 2011).

Focusing on the Kochs' direct contributions to Republican candidates also understates their role in Republican and conservative politics. As Skocpol and Hertel-Fernandez (2016) detail, the Kochs have built a large donor network and

---

[84] https://object.cato.org/sites/cato.org/files/pubs/pdf/25th_annual_report.pdf
[85] "Oil & Gas," *OpenSecrets.org*.

established Americans for Prosperity, a national organization with state-level chapters focusing on their views. The vast efforts of the Kochs have stoked partisan divisions on the environment in general and climate change in particular. Many of the corporate interests that oppose environmental regulation are not new to the GOP. Yet they are far more organized and more focused on the issue than they were in the Nixon years. So, arguably, Republican politicians were engaging in "coalition maintenance" in turning away from environmental protection. Much as Democratic MCs embraced protectionism in reaction to the pleas of their longstanding allies in organized labor when unions decided that freer trade no longer served their interests (Karol 2009), GOP legislators were heeding a new, or at least much louder message from traditional business constituencies on the environment.

As in the case of the Democrats, there have been important intracoalitional developments in the Republican Party. Other key elements of the GOP have recognized that opposition to environmental regulation is important to party constituencies. This is evident in the Christian right, which emerged as an important Republican constituency from 1980 onward. Traditionally, Christian-right leaders focused on issues like abortion, school prayer, and opposition to LGBT rights that were, at worst, orthogonal to the concerns of business interests. Even if many business interests and economic conservatives did not share all of the religious right's concerns, those did not impinge on their own agenda, making these two distinct constituencies compatible coalition partners within the GOP.

In more recent years, however, developments within the evangelical community had potentially serious implications for environmental politics. A discourse around "creation care" focusing on human stewardship over the environment became prominent in some church circles. Surveys showed some support for environmental concerns among evangelical voters (Danielsen 2013). Were this ethic to become a major focus of evangelical political concern, it would pose problems for Republicans, as it would put two key elements of their coalition at odds. Some observers wrote hopefully about this development (Billings and Samson 2012), seeing evangelicals, especially younger ones, as an untapped constituency that could shift the balance in environmental debates like climate change.

Yet as Bean and Teles (2015) detail, conservative evangelical leaders, wedded to existing alliances, worked to suppress this disruptive trend within their community. It is not hard to draw a parallel between their efforts and the resistance of environmentalist leaders in the late 1990s and early 2000s to grass-roots efforts to have the Sierra Club and other groups endorse immigration restrictions. In both cases organization leaders were embedded in a party coalition and keenly aware of the need not to raise issues that might alienate coalition partners.

A purely instrumental strategic explanation of interest group leaders' stakes in party coalitions may not be the whole story, however. Many of the staff members for these organizations work for multiple groups over the course of their careers but generally stay within the same party and ideological network. An individual might work for a party committee, on campaigns and the staffs of elected officials, in consulting, and for multiple party-aligned interest groups. Bernstein and Dominguez (2003) term the professional political operatives in this network "the expanded party."

There are many cases of important officials in leading environmental organizations who have also worked for other progressive groups or Democratic officials. Skinner (2007) notes that Margaret Conway, then Political Director of the Sierra Club, had previously worked for Planned Parenthood and the Human Rights Campaign. More recent Sierra Club Political Directors have previously worked at the AFL-CIO (Melissa Williams) and The Coalition to Stop Gun Violence, the Service Employees International Union, and Richard Gephardt's presidential campaign (Khalid Pitts). Similarly, LCV President Gene Karpinski once worked for Public Citizen and People for the American Way, and his predecessor Deb Callahan was a veteran of numerous Democratic campaigns.[86] The same pattern holds true when we look at groups antagonistic to environmentalists. Skocpol and Hertel-Fernandez (2016, 691) report in their study of the Koch brothers' Americans for Prosperity that "state directors – the paid staffers at the frontline of AFP's political operation – pursue careers that are thoroughly intertwined with the Republican Party."

To the extent that interest group leaders and senior officials are embedded professionally (and often socially) in a party network, they will tend to support interpretations of their organization's missions that reduce friction with the rest of the party. This too may be seen as instrumental for them, if not necessarily their interest group, but much research suggests that such individuals internalize the values and issue positions associated with their political party.

7.4 Peak Polarization?

Environmental issues have been part of the political agenda in Washington for decades. Divisions in this policy area, as in most others, have increasingly run along party lines. Democrats have been more supportive of environmental regulations. Yet for many years, party affiliation was *not* the only important predictor of MCs' votes on environmental issues. Both constituency measures

---

[86] http://thehill.com/policy/energy-environment/286529-sierra-club-taps-new-political-direc ted; https://content.sierraclub.org/press-releases/2015/06/sierra-club-announces-new-national-political-director; http://lcv-archive.pub30.convio.net/assets/voterguide/gene-kar pinskis-biography.html; www.bloomberg.com/research/stocks/private/person.asp? personId=82413092&privcapId=73472941&previousCapId=73472941&previousTitle=Prog ressive%20Book%20Club,LLC

and personal characteristics of legislators were strongly associated with their votes on environmental questions, even controlling for party affiliation.

Organized interests have become polarized as well. Endorsements and campaign contributions from environmental groups now overwhelmingly go to Democratic candidates, while economic interests frequently at odds with environmentalists, including fossil fuel producers and much of agribusiness, increasingly support Republicans. Divisions between Republican and Democratic voters on the environment, while not as great as among political elites, have grown as well.

In 2017, the Trump administration reversed existing policies designed to safeguard the environment. The United States withdrew from the Paris Agreement on climate change. In addition, Trump, unlike previous presidents, tried to substantially undo a proclamation of his predecessor by greatly reducing the size of a national monument Obama had established shielding large areas in Utah from development.[87]

Finally, in 2017, Republicans opened the Alaskan National Wildlife Refuge (ANWR) for oil drilling, a goal they had failed to achieve in the previous period of unified Republican government during the Bush years. In 2005, an attempt to include a provision opening up this protected area in a budget measure immune from filibuster failed, due to combined opposition from the Democratic minority and twenty-five environmentally minded GOP representatives who withheld their support until provisions opening ANWR were eliminated.[88] In 2017, however, only twelve House Republicans objected to the same proposal in the tax bill, while the GOP had a majority of twenty-four, making it easier to include this provision permitting drilling in ANWR.[89]

8 Prospects for Change

Given that all of these trends have been underway for decades, it is worth asking if they could be stopped or reversed. Two scenarios merit consideration. One theoretical possibility is that societal divisions on environmental regulation will persist, but the trend toward increasing partisanship on these issues will reverse. For such a reversal to occur, an issue of great salience that divided current party coalitions would need to emerge. It would have to be so important that many

---

[87] "Trump Slashes Size of Bears Ears and Grand Staircase Monuments," *New York Times*, December 4, 2017.

[88] "House Drops Arctic Drilling from Bill," *Washington Post*, November 10, 2005.

[89] "12 House Republicans Urge Congress to Cut ANWR Oil Drilling from Tax Bill," *Inside Climate News*, December 2, 2017, https://reichert.house.gov/press-release/reichert-fitzpatrick-and-costello-lead-letter-leadership-arctic-national-wildlife

resource use advocates and environmentalists would abandon their current party allegiances.

This seems like a remote prospect at best. Elected officials' policy stands attract interest groups and activists to party coalitions. Once inside the tent, the presence of these groups increases the incentive for parties' officeholders to pursue the policies that attracted them in the first place, sharpening parties' images and attracting more adherents who care about the policy. This is a reinforcing cycle that is not easily disrupted (Karol 2009).

Another possibility is that the current party cleavage is maintained, but that the policy debate moves substantially in one direction. There is more precedent for this scenario and, while not imminent, it is easier to imagine than the previous one. The mutual dependence between a party's politicians and its allied interest groups gives the former some leverage. A lobby often has the choice between unhappily supporting "their" party, backing a minor candidate or sitting on the sidelines – risking the election of those less favorable to their views. Defection may still make strategic sense if the group determines that it is truly being taken for granted and that its party allies could do much more for them. In such cases, the logic of temporary defection is to punish the party in the short term in hopes of gaining more reliable support in the future.

Some lobbies have used this strategy. Labor unions reduced their financial support for Democratic MCs who supported NAFTA and Permanent Normal Trade Relations with China (PNTR) (Engel and Jackson 1998, Jackson and Engel 2003). The National Rifle Association also refused to endorse George H. W. Bush for reelection in 1992 or Bob Dole for president in 1996.[90]

This is an extreme step, however, in that defectors run a great short-term risk for uncertain long-term reward. A lobby that punishes its allies risks helping elect the party less friendly to its goals and suffering whatever damage results from their time in power. Lobbies rarely do this, and even the exceptions are not always as bold as they may seem. For example, by the time the NRA announced its refusal to support George H. W. Bush in 1992 and Bob Dole four years later it was well into September and both candidates were trailing Bill Clinton by double digits in polls, making this stand on principle a less costly gesture for the gun lobby than it might have been in truly competitive races.

Usually, relations between politicians and their interest group allies do not deteriorate to such an extent. It is notable that unions opposed to NAFTA and PNTR still supported Clinton for reelection in 1996 and Gore for president in 2000, despite their promotions of these agreements. Punishing some MCs to

[90] "Staying on Sidelines in Presidential Race, NRA Snubs Dole," *New York Times*, September 18, 1996, p. A17.

make a point and deter others was one thing; alienating the president and risking GOP control of the White House was another. The NRA endorsed George W. Bush in 2000 when it was not clear that his stands on gun issues, which included nominal support for an assault weapons ban, were significantly different from those of his father or Dole.

Interest groups' reluctance to defect from their party and risk policy setbacks and access to elected officials gives the politicians with whom they are allied leverage in a two-party system. Provided they keep some distance between the other party and themselves on an issue, elected officials can move significantly in policy terms while retaining their allies' support. Some scholars even talk about the groups being "captured" by the parties, although there are disagreements about which groups are in this condition.[91]

An example illustrates this point. In the postwar years, labor unions reached the peak of their power. After a struggle to rein the unions in, culminating in the 1947 passage of the Taft-Hartley law, conflict on labor issues diminished for many years. Democrats failed to repeal Taft-Hartley, and leading Republicans came to accept unions as a permanent presence. In answering his brother Edgar, who complained in 1954 that Eisenhower had not reversed New Deal policies, the president famously argued:

> Should any political party attempt to abolish social security, unemployment insurance, and eliminate labor laws and farm programs, you would not hear of that party again in our political history. There is a tiny splinter group, of course, that believes you can do these things ... Their number is negligible and they are stupid.[92]

Eisenhower and Nixon appointed union leaders as Secretary of Labor – something it is hard to imagine a Republican president doing today. The National Labor Relations Board – paralyzed by partisan divisions and Senate deadlock over nominees in recent years – worked fairly smoothly for three decades (Moe 1987). During this era, unions remained aligned with Democrats (Greenstone 1969), while business lobbies remained close to the GOP. Yet both parties agreed that, while unions must be regulated, they were here to stay and conflict over labor issues waned.

Even in the period during which the parties have been polarized on the environment, we have seen change, albeit not the kind environmentalists are seeking. In 2008, John McCain endorsed a "cap and trade" policy to address

---

[91] Frymer (1999) saw African Americans and LGBT groups as captured by the Democratic Party, but thought other groups had avoided this status.

[92] http://web.archive.org/web/20051124190902/; www.eisenhowermemorial.org/presidential-papers/first-term/documents/1147.cfm

climate change. Yet in the next Congress he and other Republican MCs abandoned that policy (Skocpol 2013), and his successors as GOP presidential nominees, Mitt Romney and Donald Trump, rejected it as well. So even in a context of a partisan divide, the actual policies parties endorse can change. If public concern about the environment were sufficient, Republican politicians could tell corporate donors that concessions to the public mood are necessary.

Most Republicans are not interested in that exercise at present. There are some reasons, however, why significant change in the Republican position – or at least that of a significant number of GOP politicians is imaginable in years to come.

8.1 A Republican Coalition in Demographic Decline

Republicans gained control of the entire federal government in 2016. Yet they achieved this only because their vote was efficiently distributed across states and districts. This political geography allowed them to expand their Senate majority in 2018 even as they lost control of the House. The GOP has won the popular vote in a presidential election only once since the end of the Cold War. They have also gained control of Congress while receiving fewer votes than their opponents, as was the case for the House of Representatives in 2012.

Republican support is concentrated in shrinking demographics: older and evangelical whites. Whites were 81 percent percent of voters in 2000, but only 70 percent in 2016. Trump won a higher share of the white vote than George W. Bush (58 percent vs. 55 percent) but lost the popular vote by a wider margin and only won the electoral college because his votes were distributed so efficiently. If racial polarization results in the GOP finding increased support among the shrinking white majority, favorable electoral geography and vote suppression tactics might allow them to remain competitive in the medium term.

Yet while the political power of racial division should never be underestimated, it is not clear this is a winning long-term strategy given the party loyalties of different age cohorts. Until recently, age was not an important predictor of vote choice. In 2000, Al Gore actually did slightly better than George W. Bush with voters over 50.[93]

In the 2004 election, however, an age gap emerged as Bush won 52 percent among voters over 65, but only 43 percent among those 25 and under. In 2016 Donald Trump also won 52 percent among the 65 and older cohort, but only 36 percent among voters 25 and under.[94] In part, the age gap reflects the greater

[93] https://ropercenter.cornell.edu/polls/us-elections/how-groups-voted/how-groups-voted-2000/
[94] https://ropercenter.cornell.edu/polls/us-elections/how-groups-voted/how-groups-voted-2004/;
https://ropercenter.cornell.edu/polls/us-elections/how-groups-voted/groups-voted-2016/

racial diversity of younger cohorts. Yet even among whites the young are less supportive of Republicans than their elders. Trump won whites over 65 by 19 points and those under 30 by only four.[95]

The core GOP constituency of white evangelicals is also aging. From 2007 to 2014, the share of white evangelicals over 50 increased from 48 to 54 percent. White evangelicals went from 21 percent of the public in 2006 to only 17 percent in 2016.[96]

In short, Republicans rely on declining demographics. They have won narrow victories based on favorable political geography in presidential and congressional elections. Eventually, this will no longer be possible. While Trump has been especially unpopular with younger cohorts, these demographic trends predate his election.

Parties tend to adapt only after repeated defeat. Moreover, even if, following some losses, Republicans do eventually revisit policy commitments, there is no guarantee that the environment is where they would start. This is only one possibility.

Yet if Republicans are to remain competitive, they will eventually have to adapt. There is precedent for them doing so in the environmental policy area. As Manik Roy notes, even as the parties have polarized in recent decades, leading Republicans in political trouble have periodically shown concern for the environment. These actions did not alter the basic party alignment on the issue, but they were consequential in policy terms.[97] Policy changes on the environment might actually prove easier for Republicans than modifying stands on issues like immigration, which connects directly to identity politics.

8.2 Younger GOP Voters Are More Pro-Environment

While a party base in demographic decline can be addressed in multiple ways, there is logic to adopting a more progressive position on climate change in response. Studies have long shown that younger voters are more supportive of environmental regulations than their elders. This relationship can be explained in multiple ways.

Some element of this gap may be a life-cycle effect; younger people's longer time horizon gives them more reason to worry about the future. If this were the whole story, the GOP could count on younger voters to care less about the environment as they age. Yet there is reason to believe a cohort effect also

[95] www.cnn.com/election/results/exit-polls
[96] www.pewforum.org/religious-landscape-study/religious-tradition/evangelical-protestant/racial-and-ethnic-composition/white/; www.pewforum.org/religious-landscape-study/religious-tradition/evangelical-protestant/racial-and-ethnic-composition/white/
[97] "It's Not Too Late to 'Go Green' in Changing Climate of Washington," *The Hill*, May 31, 2017.

exists. Millennials and postmillennials were raised in an era in which the problem of climate change was widely discussed. This is far less true of baby boomers and their remaining elders. Each new generation grows up in a world in which environmental concerns are important and is likely to retain this perspective.

Surveys reveal a generation gap even among Republicans on environmental issues, especially the subject of climate change.[98] A recent survey of college Republican clubs found widespread recognition that climate change was a result of human activity, along with openness to solutions.[99] While the public has increasingly divided along party lines about climate change, this is less true of younger cohorts. According to a recent study, 57 percent of Republican and Republican-leaning millennials believe that there is "solid evidence" of climate change. While 94 percent of millennial Democrats believe this, it is notable that majorities on both sides share this understanding. By contrast most GOP baby boomers and members of the pre-boomer "Silent Generation" do not accept that there is solid evidence, putting them at odds with overwhelming majorities of Democrats within their age groups.[100]

8.3 The Declining Fossil Fuel Sector

Turning from demographics to interest groups reveals that Republicans are wedded to a shrinking constituency here as well: the fossil fuel sector. Given the centrality of fossil fuel interests in resisting action on climate change, a decline in the power of this industry could lead to a depolarization of the issue or possibly a continuing debate, albeit shifted toward action.

Employment in coal mining has dropped by roughly two-thirds – from 150,000 to 50,000 in the last thirty years.[101] Employment in oil and gas production, however, has dropped only from 199,000 to 178,000. In addition, while coal has long been in decline, there has been a resurgence of oil and gas employment, as natural gas fracking has increased. The oil and gas sector bottomed out at around 120,000 jobs in 2003, and has since rebounded. Still, given the growth in the American workforce (a 35 percent increase since 1987, according to the BLS), fossil fuel accounts for a declining share of overall employment.

---

[98] www.washingtonpost.com/news/wonk/wp/2014/11/19/the-polls-are-clear-younger-republi
cans-support-action-on-climate-change/
[99] www.reuters.com/article/us-climatechange-politics-youth-feature/in-generational-shift-col
lege-republicans-poised-to-reform-party-on-climate-change-idUSKBN17E2XF
[100] www.people-press.org/2018/03/01/4-race-immigration-same-sex-marriage-abortion-global-
warming-gun-policy-marijuana-legalization/
[101] https://data.bls.gov/pdq/

In both cases, these figures may be too low because they do not include those employed in support of energy production, such as coal truck drivers.[102] Moreover, many people not directly employed in fossil fuel production may feel a stake in these industries, including those in the service sector in areas dependent on this industry, and even homeowners in those communities whose property values depend on the fortunes of local firms. Yet even if they understate the weight of the sector in an absolute sense, there is no reason to doubt that the Bureau of Labor Statistics captures the trend, revealing an industry that is important to the livelihood of a declining share of Americans.[103]

While the fossil fuel sector makes up a shrinking share of the economy, however, it remains a major player in campaign finance. Campaign contributions from oil and gas producers grew from $12,347,640 to $104,802,263 from 1990 to 2016, while coal interests' campaign spending increased from $888,819 to $13,497,867 in the same period.[104] This represents more than a quadrupling of oil and gas contributions in real terms, while campaign funds from the coal sector have grown more than eightfold.

Further context is gained by comparing the growth in contributions by fossil fuel producers to that in campaigns generally. In 1990, $408.5 million was spent on congressional races.[105] By 2016, spending had grown nearly tenfold to $4.05 billion. Much of this increase was Super PAC and independent expenditures. All in all, fossil fuel producers spent 5.4 times as much in 2016 as they had in 1990, correcting for inflation.

So while the fossil fuel industry employs a shrinking proportion of the electorate, this sector has more than kept up with the great increase in campaign contributions in recent decades. In the short term, money may compensate for declining numbers, but that is not a tactic that can be employed indefinitely in the face of organized opposition and hostile public opinion.

For example, the tobacco industry has long had a well-funded lobby. Yet from the 1964 Surgeon General's warning onward, cigarette producers suffered defeat after defeat. Firms were required to print health warnings on cigarette boxes and later to strengthen the warnings. Cigarette ads were banned from television. Smoking was banned on airlines. The Food and Drug Administration was given authority to regulate tobacco (Derthick 2012). Local ordinances banned smoking in public places. Cigarette taxes were adopted and increased (Marshall 2016).

---

[102] "Are Coal Mining Jobs up by 50,000 since Last Year? Not Exactly," *Politifact*, June 5, 2017.
[103] The growth of gas fracking and shale-based fuel could reverse this trend, even if coal's decline continues, however.
[104] Center for Responsive Politics at www.opensecrets.org/industries/totals.php?cycle=2018&ind=E1210
[105] www.brookings.edu/wp-content/uploads/2016/06/Vital-Statistics-Chapter-3-Campaign-Finance-in-Congressional-Elections.pdf

The antismoking struggle was protracted, and tobacco producers' wealth no doubt enabled them to delay some measures or to limit their scope. Yet while they fought a long holding action and even won some battles, "Big Tobacco" lost the war. From 1965 to 2014, the share of smokers in the population shrank from 42.4 percent to 16.8 percent.[106] Tobacco producers split politically, with the largest firm, Phillip Morris, eventually viewing FDA regulation as the lesser evil (Derthick 2012). This example is relevant for those interested in climate change, since the tobacco industry was also contending with scientific findings and public opinion.

8.4 Renewable Energy as a Counterbalance?

Another part of the story is the growing role of the renewable energy sector. In percentage terms, the growth in campaign contributions by renewable producers is enormous. The Center for Responsive Politics found that this sector gave a negligible $87,189 to federal campaigns in 1990. By 2016, however, the renewable sector contributed $3,967,149. Even adjusting for inflation, this sector is now giving nearly twenty-five times more than it did in 1990. Yet while this trend is impressive, the renewable sector is still a minor player in campaign finance compared to fossil fuel producers.

Not only is the renewable sector a growing source of campaign funds, however, unlike environmentalists it also directs a significant share of its support to Republicans. In 2016, 36 percent of contributions from renewable producers went to GOP candidates. In the 2014 cycle, 42 percent did. The analogous figures for environment-minded donors were 3 percent for 2016 and 7 percent for 2014.[107] If the renewable sector continues to grow, it could counterbalance fossil fuel producers and bolster Republicans who diverge from the party line on climate.

8.5 Building Credibility and Winning Attention: An Opportunity for Farsighted Republican Politicians

Republican officials who believe that human activity contributes to climate change should also believe that this fact will become increasingly evident. If so, farsighted Republicans might see an advantage in building credibility on the issue. Some candidates have benefitted by getting ahead of the curve. Barack Obama's opposition to the Iraq War in 2002 helped him defeat Hillary Clinton in the 2008 Democratic primaries, even though their voting records on Iraq were identical once Obama reached the US Senate. GOP politicians taking strong stands on climate change are also more newsworthy than Democrats doing the same. So Republicans

[106] "Who Still Smokes in the U.S. in Seven Simple Charts," *Washington Post,* November 12, 2015.
[107] www.opensecrets.org/industries/totals.php?cycle=2018&ind=E1500; www.opensecrets.org/industries/totals.php?cycle=2018&ind=Q11

who differentiate themselves from their party on this issue could reap rewards in terms of media coverage.

Yet politicians must worry about the short term, or they will not reach the long term. There are reasons why Republican candidates and officeholders hesitate before breaking ranks on climate change or other issues. For most the primary, not the general election, is their greatest point of vulnerability. GOP moderates and even conservatives have lost primaries since the rise of the Tea Party a decade ago. For every rebel who is successfully "primaried," several potential rebels are deterred.

Yet an incumbent seldom loses a primary based on a single stand. One case sometimes cited is former Rep. Bob Inglis of South Carolina. Inglis supported addressing climate change, albeit via a carbon tax rather than the "cap and trade" plan that passed the House in 2009. He was subsequently badly defeated in the 2010 primary. Yet Inglis had given his GOP opponents much more ammunition, voting for the 2008 "bailout" of the financial sector and opposing the surge of troops in Iraq in 2007.[108]

8.6 Green Shoots? The Climate Solutions Caucus

There are some signs of movement among Republicans. In the 114th Congress, a bipartisan caucus was founded in the House of Representatives to address climate change. As of October 2018, the Climate Solutions Caucus had 45 Democratic and 45 Republican members.[109] These MCs supported – at least in theory – action to address climate change. Climate Solutions Caucus members made up just over one-sixth of the House Republican Conference and it is worth focusing on them to see whether they may be the beginnings of something more.

Fifteen of the 43 Republican Representatives in this caucus in the fall of 2018 represented districts Hillary Clinton won in 2016.[110] Given that Clinton won only 23 districts represented by GOP MCs in the 115th Congress, cross-pressured Republicans were greatly overrepresented in the Caucus. It is also notable that of the 28 other GOP Caucus members, nine were freshmen. (None of those from districts Clinton won are freshmen.) In short, a majority of GOP Climate Solutions Caucus members were drawn from two small subsets of the Republican Conference. Another measure tells a similar tale. GOP MCs identified by the Cook Political Report in August 2018 as representing vulnerable districts were about three times as likely as their copartisans to be members of the Climate Solutions Caucus.[111]

---

[108] www.motherjones.com/politics/2010/08/bob-inglis-tea-party-casualty/
[109] https://citizensclimatelobby.org/climate-solutions-caucus/
[110] www.dailykos.com/stories/2017/2/6/1629653/-Daily-Kos-Elections-2016-presidential-results-for-congressional-and-legislative-districts
[111] https://twitter.com/Redistrict/status/1027680768552853510

The GOP caucus members had a distinctive geographical profile as well. Twenty-six of 43 representatives were from east or west coast states.[112] Only nine were from the south, and all but two of those were from Florida and Virginia. Three were from south Florida, which is geographically, but not politically, southern. One was from a Virginia district that includes Washington, DC suburbs. The remaining two were from Florida and Virginia, districts with long coastlines. Finally, one represented a coastal district in the Charleston area. Among southern Republican Caucus members, only a Kentucky MC represented a district far from the coast.

Finally, interest in climate change did *not* reflect a larger environmental consciousness on the part of most GOP Caucus members. Brian Fitzpatrick, a Republican freshman from suburban Philadelphia, had the highest rating at 71. Fitzpatrick was the only GOP Caucus member to vote with the LCV even half of the time. The median LCV rating among Republican Climate Solutions Caucus members for the first session of the 115th Congress is 9. Caucus members took varied positions on President Trump's decision to withdraw from the Paris Agreement. A letter from the cochairs urging Trump to remain in the accord was signed by only three GOP Caucus members.[113]

Twenty-eight of 34 GOP representatives who were then Caucus members[114] voted for the 2017 tax bill, which opened up ANWR to drilling, a long-time goal of oil producers. Ten Caucus members and two other Republican MCs wrote to leaders urging them not to include the opening of ANWR in the tax bill.[115] Given the lack of Democratic support for the bill, GOP Caucus members working as a bloc might have gotten the ANWR provision removed. Yet five of the ten letter signatories voted for the tax bill. The seven GOP no votes from the Caucus were all from New York, New Jersey, and California – states in which the bill's provisions regarding state and local tax deductibility were unpopular.[116]

For those hoping for a shift in GOP positioning on climate change, these MCs presented a mixed picture. The fact that their districts were so atypical for Republicans suggests that they are unlikely to be joined by many others soon. Their mixed response to Trump's withdrawal from the Paris Accord and the opening of ANWR along with their low LCV ratings led environmentalists to

---

[112] GOP caucus members also include the nonvoting delegates from American Samoa and Puerto Rico. These delegates are not rated by the LCV.

[113] https://pilotonline.com/news/government/nation/months-in-rep-scott-taylor-is-trying-to-ele vate-his/article_6e3d5b1b-b846-5c61-bd1c-a1644f839ca4.html; https://curbelo.house.gov/ news/documentsingle.aspx?DocumentID=1441

[114] The ranks of the Caucus grew after the tax bill passed.

[115] "12 House Republicans Urge Congress to Cut ANWR Oil Drilling from Tax Bill," *Inside Climate News*, December 2, 2007, https://reichert.house.gov/press-release/reichert-fitzpatrick-and-costello-lead-letter-leadership-arctic-national-wildlife

[116] https://thinkprogress.org/republican-climate-members-vote-656c69f72991/

question their seriousness. A Sierra Club spokeswoman asserted that GOP Climate Solutions Caucus members "are finding an easy action to get a green badge or a line on their resumes." Similarly, Gene Karpinski, the President of the League of Conservation Voters, said, "[T]hey may sign up for the caucus and claim to care about the environment, but their voting records speak very differently."[117]

The 2018 midterm election was devastating for GOP Climate Solutions Caucus members. Twenty-two or nearly half of them did not return to the 116th Congress. Eight retired, in some cases facing uphill races for reelection, while fourteen others, including caucus cofounder Carlos Curbelo, were defeated.[118] These results could be seen as evidence that support for the environment offers Republicans no electoral benefits. Many GOP MCs attracted to the Caucus, however, were already in vulnerable positions. It is typically moderates in swing districts who pay the price when their party loses favor.

While climate change activists hope for broad-based bipartisan support, even a small number of GOP MCs could make a large difference. In 2005–2006 two dozen House Republicans kept provisions opening ANWR out of a budget measure, a step that preserved that refuge for more than a decade. Similarly, the eight Republican MCs who voted for cap and trade in 2009 were pivotal in that bill's passage in the House, given the opposition of Democrats from fossil-fuel-producing districts. There are still important differences among Republicans that roll-call-based ratings may not reveal. The recent GOP-controlled 115th Congress rejected the Trump Administration's proposal to cut EPA funding by one-third, for example (Turner and Isenberg 2018, 213).

If there is to be a substantial policy response to climate change, it will stem in part from actions by politicians who have not always pleased environmentalists. Historic changes have occurred when leaders whose records were far from pure adapted to new political conditions. Lyndon Johnson's leading role in the enactment of civil rights laws is the most dramatic example, given his long support for Jim Crow. More recently, support for same-sex marriage went from being a fringe position to a mainstream one via its adoption by many leading politicians including Barack Obama, Joe Biden, and Hillary Clinton, none of whom supported it a decade ago.

The 2018 elections dealt a severe blow to the Climate Solutions Caucus Republicans. Yet the overrepresentation of freshmen among the GOP Caucus

---

[117] "A Climate Caucus Has Turned into a Magnet for Republicans. Wait, What?," *Mother Jones*, February 15, 2018; "LCV's Gene Karpinski Guards the 'Green Firewall' in Congress," *E&E News*, May 25, 2018.
[118] "Midterms Wash Away Nearly Half of Climate Caucus Republicans," *Roll Call*, November 8, 2018.

members suggested that growing numbers of new Republican MCs will think that at least showing concern about this issue is advisable. For now, joining a caucus could be a sufficient gesture in their eyes, but it may not end there. The answers to the questions of how serious the small minority of Congressional Republicans who have spoken up on climate change really are, and whether others will join them, may depend on how much pressure is brought to bear.

9 Conclusions

The politics of the environment in the United States have become highly partisan. Environmental groups, while formally nonpartisan, are now closely aligned with the Democratic Party. Fossil fuel producers and other economic interests that clash with environmentalists overwhelmingly support the GOP. Republican Members of Congress are now far more likely than Democrats to represent constituencies in which resource extraction is a key part of the local economy. Under Republican leadership the United States is a global outlier in rejecting the Paris Agreement.

In this Element I placed American environmental politics in comparative perspective, explaining why the United States has no important Green Party and why Democrats and Republicans have diverged on environmental issues. While many controversies have become partisan in contemporary American politics, environmental issues have their own distinctive history. I documented the transformation of the nonpartisan Progressive Era conservation movement concerned about efficiency and characterized by racist and eugenicist beliefs into the modern environmental movement: a key component of the Democratic Party aligned with feminists, racial and sexual minorities, and labor unions. Polarization occurred not only in Washington but also at the state level, albeit with important variation across states. Environmentalism has not been a constant but has come to include opposition to nuclear power not present in the early years of that technology, as well as growing concern about climate change.

The case of environmental politics highlights two broader dynamics interesting to students of party position change. Firstly, when this new issue arose, the reactions of legislators in Washington and state capitals were linked to the same characteristics that were associated with voter attitudes: age and education. Both younger and better-educated legislators and ordinary citizens supported environmental regulation. Yet nowadays these personal characteristics matter far more among voters than elected officials. Politicians, more than voters, have incentives to take positions in line with the preferences of all key elements of their party coalition.

Secondly, the study shows how interest groups both influence parties and are in turn influenced by them. The parties' polarization on environmental issues owes much to the effective incorporation of groups like the Sierra Club and League of Conservation Voters in the ranks of the Democratic Party, and the strengthened organizational presence of fossil fuel and development interests in the GOP. Environmental organizations were reluctant partisans, yet once in a party coalition they had a clear political incentive to take the preferences of coalition partners into account. Nowadays many leading officials in environmental organizations have work experience in other progressive interest groups and/or spent time on the staff of Democratic officials, campaigns, or party committees.

Thus the Sierra Club – long a very white organization – embraced diversity and "environmental justice" concerns and, most dramatically, beat back grassroots efforts to make it an anti-immigration lobby. Labor unions have tempered their disagreements with environmentalists on development issues. Environmentalists have in turn joined unions in opposing trade agreements, and both groups are increasingly supportive of immigration. In the Republican Party conservative evangelical leaders pushed back against the "creation care" movement, which would have brought them into conflict with fossil fuel interests that were their partners in the GOP.

Once established, party-interest group alignments are sticky. Yet there are some reasons to believe that Republicans may eventually reconsider their stand on the environment. Their votes come mostly from aging demographics, and younger voters are more concerned about the environment. The renewable energy sector is expanding rapidly, while coal is in decline. GOP Members of Congress in marginal seats showed that they thought it useful to be associated with concern about climate change, although it saved few in 2018.

If public concern about climate change increases and Republicans fare badly in elections, GOP elected officials may decide they need to change course, and the environment is one area in which they could do so. Yet whether this would reduce the current gap between the parties would depend on the stands Democrats took. If Democrats took stronger stands on the environment than they do today, polarization might continue, but with policy outcomes more reflective of environmentalists' concerns as politicians in both parties move in the same direction. Whether or not today's party alignment on the environment endures, it has already had real policy consequences, making examination of its origins worthwhile.

References

Achen, Christopher H. and Larry Bartels. 2016. *Democracy for Realists: Why Elections Don't Produce Responsive Government*. Princeton: Princeton University Press.

Adams, Greg D. 1997. "Abortion: Evidence of an Issue Evolution." *American Journal of Political Science*. Vol. 41 No. 3: 718–737.

Bawn, Kathleen, Martin Cohen, David Karol, Seth Masket, Hans Noel, and John Zaller. 2012. "A Theory of Political Parties: Groups, Policy Demands and Nominations in American Politics." *Perspectives on Politics*. Vol. 10 No. 3: 571–597.

Baylor, Christopher. 2018. *First to the Party: The Group Origins of Political Transformation*. Philadelphia: University of Pennsylvania Press.

Bean, Lydia and Steven M. Teles. 2015. *Spreading the Gospel of Climate Change: An Evangelical Battleground*. Washington DC: New America Foundation.

Bernstein, Jonathan and Casey B. K. Dominguez. 2003. "Candidates and Candidacies in the Expanded Party." *P.S. Political Science & Politics*. Vol. 36 No. 2: 165–169

Billings, Dwight B. and Will Samson. 2012 "Evangelical Christians and the Environment: "Christians for the Mountains" and the Appalachian Movement against Mountaintop Removal Coal Mining." *Worldviews*. Vol. 16 No. 1: 1–29.

Binder, Sarah A. and Forrest Maltzman. 2002. "Senatorial Delay in Confirming Federal Judges, 1947–1998." *American Journal of Political Science*. Vol. 46 No. 1: 190–199.

Bishin, Benjamin G. 2009. *Tyranny of the Minority: The Subconstituency Theory of Representation*. Philadelphia: Temple University Press.

Bishop, Bill G. and Robert Cushing. 2008. *The Big Sort: Why the Clustering of Like-Minded America is Tearing Us Apart*. New York: Houghton Mifflin Harcourt.

Brooks, Karl. 2009. *Public Power, Private Dams: The Hells Canyon High Dam Controversy*. Seattle: University of Washington Press.

Burnham, Walter Dean. 1970. *Critical Elections and the Mainsprings of American Politics*. New York: Norton.

Carmines, Edward and James Stimson. 1989. *Issue Evolution: Race and the Transformation of American Politics*. Princeton: Princeton University Press.

Carnes, Nicholas. 2013. *White-Collar Government. The Hidden Role of Class in Economic Policy Making*. Chicago: University of Chicago Press.

Carter, Neil. 2013. "Greening the Mainstream: Party Politics and the Environment." *Environmental Politics*. Vol. 22 No. 1: 73–94.

Chen, Anthony S. 2009. *The Fifth Freedom: Jobs, Politics and Civil Rights in the United States, 1941–1972*. Princeton: Princeton University Press.

Clarke, Alice. 2001. "The Sierra Club and Immigration Policy: A Critique." Politics and the Life Sciences. 19–28.

Cohen, Marty, David Karol, Hans Noel, and John Zaller. 2008. *The Party Decides: Parties before and after Reform*. Chicago: University of Chicago Press.

Curry, James M. and Frances E. Lee. 2019. "Non-Party Government: Bipartisan Lawmaking and Party Power in Congress." *Perspectives on Politics*. Vol. 17 No. 1:47-65.

Dalton, Russell J. 2009. "Economics, Environmentalism and Party Alignments: A Note on Partisan Change in Advanced Industrial Democracies." *European Journal of Political Research*. Vol. 48 No. 2: 161–175.

Danielsen, Sabrina. 2013. "Fracturing Over Creation Care? Shifting Environmental Beliefs among Evangelicals, 1984–2010." *Journal for the Scientific Study of Religion*. Vol. 52 No. 1: 198–215.

Dark, Taylor E. 2001. *The Unions and Democrats: An Enduring Alliance*. Ithaca: Cornell University Press.

Derthick, Martha. 2012. "From Litigation to Legislation: The Surrender of Phillip Morris." *Political Science Quarterly*. Vol. 127 No. 3: 401–415.

Dominguez, Casey and Richard Skinner. 2014. "Friends and Family: A Sketch of Group-Party Alliance Over Time." Paper Presented at the 2014 Annual Meeting of the American Political Science Association, August 27–31, Washington DC.

Dunlap, Riley E. and Michael Patrick Allen. 1976. "Partisan Differences on Environmental Issues: A Congressional Roll-Call Analysis." *Western Political Quarterly*. Vol. 29 No. 3: 384–397.

Dunlap, Riley and Aaron McCright, 2011. "Organized Climate Change Denial." In John S. Dryzek, Richard Norgaard and David Schosberg, eds., *Oxford Handbook of Climate Change and Society*. New York: Oxford University Press.

Egan, Patrick J. and Megan Mullin. 2017. "Climate Change: US Public Opinion" *Annual Review of Political Science*. Vol. 20: 209–227.

Engel, Steven T. and David J. Jackson. 1998. "Wielding the Stick instead of the Carrot: Labor PAC Punishment of Pro-NAFTA Democrats." *Political Research Quarterly*. Vol. 51 No. 3: 813–828.

Feinstein, Brian D. and Eric Schickler. 2008. Platforms and Partners: The Civil Rights Realignment Reconsidered. *Studies in American Political Development*. Vol. 22 No. 1: 1–31.

Fenno, Richard F. Jr. 1978. *Home Style: House Members in their Districts.* Boston: Little, Brown.

Fisher, Dana R. 2004. *National Governance and the Global Climate Change Regime.* Lanham, MD: Rowman & Littlefield.

Flippen, J. Brooks. 2000. *Nixon and the Environment.* Albuquerque: University of New Mexico Press.

Fox, Steven R. 1981. *The American Conservation Movement: John Muir and his Legacy.* Boston: Little, Brown.

Frymer, Paul. 1999. *Uneasy Alliances: Race and Party Competition in America.* Princeton: Princeton University Press.

Gamson, William A. and Andre Modigliani. 1989. "Media Discourse and Public Opinion on Nuclear Power: A Constructivist Approach." *American Journal of Sociology.* Vol. 95 No. 1: 1–37.

Gelpi, Christopher and Peter Feaver. 2002. "Speak Softly and Carry a Big Stick? Veterans in the Political Elite and the American Use of Force." *American Political Science Review.* Vol. 96 No. 4: 779–793.

Greenstone, J. David. 1969. *Labor in American Politics.* New York: Knopf.

Grose, Christian, R. 2011. *Congress in Black and White: Race and Representation in Washington and at Home.* New York: Cambridge University Press.

Grumbach, Jacob M. 2018. "From Backwaters to Major Policymakers: Policy Polarization in the States, 1970–2014." *Perspectives on Politics.* Vol. 6: 416–435.

Hadden, Jennifer. 2015. *Networks in Contention: The Divisive Politics of Climate Change.* New York: Cambridge University Press.

Harris, Robert J. 1953. "States' Rights and Vested Interests." *Journal of Politics.* Vol. 15 No. 4: 457–471.

Hays, Samuel. 1959. *Conservation and the Gospel of Efficiency: The Progressive Conservation Movement: 1890–1920.* Cambridge: Harvard University Press.

Hinchcliffe, Kelsey L. and Frances E. Lee. 2016. "Party Competition and Conflict in State Legislatures." *State Politics and Policy Quarterly.* Vol. 16 No. 2: 172–197.

Hofstadter, Richard. 1955. *The Age of Reform.* New York: Vintage.

Hopkins, David A. 2017. *Red Fighting Blue: How Geography and Electoral Rules Polarize American Politics.* New York: Cambridge University Press.

Inglehart, Ronald. 1995. "Public Support for Environmental Protection: Objective Problems and Subjective Values in 43 Societies" *PS- Political Science & Politics.* Vol. 28 No. 1: 57–72.

Jackson, David J. and Steven T. Engel. 2003. "Friends Don't Let Friends Vote for Free Trade: The Dynamics of the Labor PAC Punishment Strategy over PNTR." *Political Research Quarterly*. Vol. 56 No. 4: 441–448.

Kalman, Laura. 2017. *The Long Reach of the Sixties: LBJ, Nixon and the Making of the Contemporary Supreme Court*. New York: Oxford University Press.

Kamienicki, Sheldon. 1995. "Political Parties and Environmental Policy." In James P. Lester, ed., *Environmental Politics and Policy: Theories and Evidence*. Durham: Duke University Press.

Karol, David. 2009. *Party Position Change in American Politics: Coalition Management*. New York: Cambridge University Press.

Karol, David. 2014. "Parties Revised and Revived: Democrats and Republicans in the Age of Reagan." In Marjorie Hershey, ed., *CQ Press Guide to U.S. Political Parties*. Thousand Oaks: CQ Press.

Karol, David. 2015. "Party Activists, Interest Groups and Polarization in American Politics." In James A. Thurber and Antoine Yoshinaka, eds., *American Gridlock: The Sources, Character and Impact of Political Polarization*. New York: Cambridge University Press.

Karol, David and Chloe Thurston. 2014. "From Personal to Partisan: Abortion, Party and Religion in the California State Assembly, 1967–2000." Paper presented at the 2014 Annual Meeting of the European Political Science Association. June 19–21, Edinburgh, Scotland.

King, Leslie. 2008. "Ideology, Strategy and Conflict in a Social Movement Organization: The Sierra Club Immigration Wars." *Mobilization: The International Quarterly*. Vol. 13 No.1: 45–61.

Klyza, Christopher McGrory and David J. Sousa. 2013. *American Environmental Policy: Beyond Gridlock*. Cambridge: MIT Press.

Kousser, Thad. 2009. "How Geopolitics Cleaved California's Republicans and United its Democrats." *California Journal of Politics and Policy*. Vol. 1 No. 1: 2–15.

Layman, Geoffrey C., Thomas M. Carsey, John C. Green, Richard Herrera, Rosalyn Cooperman. 2010. "Activists and Conflict Extension in American Politics." *American Political Science Review*. Vol. 104 No. 2: 324–347.

Layzer, Judith A. 2012. *Open for Business: Conservatives' Opposition to Environmental Regulation*. Cambridge: MIT Press.

Lenz, Gabriel. 2012. *Follow the Leader? How Voters Respond to Politicians' Policies and Performance*. Chicago: University of Chicago Press.

Lockwood, Matthew. 2018. "Right-Wing Populism and the Climate Change Agenda: Exploring the Linkages." *Environmental Politics*. Vol. 27 No.4: 712–732.

Marshall, Thomas. 2016. *Public Opinion, Public Policy, and Smoking: The Transformation of American Attitudes and Cigarette Use, 1890–2016*. Lanham, MD: Lexington Books.

Mayhew, David R. 1974. *Congress: The Electoral Connection*. New Haven: Yale University Press.

Mayhew, David R. 1986. *Placing Parties in American Politics: Organization, Electoral Settings and Government Activity in the Twentieth Century*. Princeton: Princeton University Press.

Mayhew, David R. 2004. *Electoral Realignments: A Critique of an American Genre*. New Haven: Yale University Press.

McCright, Aaron M. and Riley. E. Dunlap. 2011. "The Politicization of Climate Change and Polarization of the American Public's Views of Global Warming, 2001–2010." *Sociological Quarterly*. Vol. 52 No. 2: 155–194.

McGirr, Lisa. 2015. *The War on Alcohol: Prohibition and the Rise of the American State*. New York: W. W. Norton.

McTague, John and Shana Pearson-Merkowitz. 2013. "Voting from the Pew; The Effect of Senators' Religious Identities on Partisan Polarization in the U.S. Senate." *Legislative Studies Quarterly*. Vol. 38: 405–430.

Meyer, John M. 1997. "Gifford Pinchot, John Muir and the Boundaries of Politics in American Thought." *Polity*. Vol. 30. No. 2: 267–284.

Miler, Kristina C. 2010. *Constituency Representation in Congress: The View from the Hill*. New York: Cambridge University Press.

Miller, Warren E. and Donald W. Stokes. 1963. "Constituency Influence in Congress." *American Political Science Review*. Vol. 57: 45–46.

Mitchell, Robert Cameron, Angela G. Mertig, and Riley E. Dunlap. 1991. "Twenty Years of Environmental Mobilization: Trends among National Environmental Organizations." *Society and Natural Resources*. Vol. 4: 219–234.

Moe, Terry. 1987. "Interests, Institutions and Positive Theory: The Politics of the NLRB." *Studies in American Political Development*. Vol. 2: Spring 236–299.

Obach, Brian K. 2002. "Labor-Environmental Relations: An Analysis of the Relationship between Labor Unions and Environmentalists." *Social Science Quarterly*. Vol. 83 No. 1: 82–100.

Obach, Brian K. 2004. *Labor and the Environmental Movement: The Quest for Common Ground*. Cambridge: MIT Press.

Ogarzalek, Thomas. 2018. *Cities on the Hill: How Urban Institutions Transform National Politics*. New York: Oxford University Press.

Poole, Keith. 1988. "Recent Developments in Analytical Models of Voting in the U.S. Congress." *Legislative Studies Quarterly*. Vol. 13 No.1: 117–133.

Poole, Keith and Howard Rosenthal. 2007. *Ideology and Congress: A Political-Economic History of Roll Call Voting*. Transaction Publishers: Piscataway.

Richardson, Elmo R. 1958. "Conservation as a Political Issue: The Western Progressives' Political Dilemma, 1909–1912." *The Pacific Northwest Quarterly*. Vol. 49 No.2: 49–54.

Schickler, Eric. 2016. *Racial Realignment: The Transformation of American Liberalism, 1932–1965*. Princeton: Princeton University Press.

Scherer, Nancy. 2005. *Scoring Points: Politicians, Activists and the Lower Federal Court Appointment Process*. Palo Alto: Stanford University Press.

Schlozman, Daniel. 2015. *When Movements Anchor Parties: Electoral Alignments in American History*. Princeton: Princeton University Press.

Schrepfer, Susan R. 1992. "The Nuclear Crucible: Diablo Canyon and the Transformation of the Sierra Club." *California History*. Vol. 71 No. 2: 212–237.

Scott, James. 1999. *Seeing Like a State: How Certain Schemes to Improve the Human Condition Have Failed*. New Haven: Yale University Press.

Shoch, James. 2001. *Trading Blows: Party Competition and U.S. Trade Policy in a Globalizing Era*. Chapel Hill: University of North Carolina Press.

Shor, Boris. 2015. "Polarization in American State Legislatures." In James Thurber and Antoine Yoshinaka, eds., *American Gridlock: The Sources, Character and Impact of Political Polarization*.

Skinner, Richard. 2007. *More Than Money: Interest Group Action in Congressional Elections*. Lanham, MD: Rowman & Littlefield.

Skocpol, Theda. 2013. "Naming The Problem: What It Will Take to Counter Extremism and Engage Americans in the Fight against Global Warming." Prepared for the Symposium on The Politics of America's Fight Against Global Warming Co-sponsored by the Columbia School of Journalism and the Scholars Strategy Network. February 14, 2013. Tsai Auditorium, Harvard University.

Skocpol, Theda and Alexander Hertel-Fernandez. 2016. "The Koch Network and Republican Party Extremism." *Perspectives on Politics*. Vol. 14 No.3: 681–700.

Spiro, Jonathan Peter. 2008. *Defending the Master Race: Conservation, Eugenics and the Legacy of Madison Grant*. Lebanon, NH: University of Vermont Press.

Stokes, Leah C. and Christopher Warshaw. 2017. "Renewable Energy Policy Design and Framing Influence Public Support in the United States." *Nature Energy 2* No. 8: 17107.

Sundquist, James L. 1983. *Dynamics of the Party System: Alignment and Realignment of Political Parties in the United States*. Washington, DC: Brookings Institution.

Swers, Michele. 2005. "Connecting Descriptive and Substantive Representation: An Analysis of Sex Differences in Cosponsorship Activity." *Legislative Studies Quarterly.* Vol. 30 No. 3: 407–433.

Thomsen, Danielle M. 2017. *Opting Out of Congress: Partisan Polarization and the Decline of Moderate Candidates.* New York: Cambridge University Press.

Turner, James Morton. 2009. "'The Specter of Environmentalism': Wilderness, Environmental Politics, and the Evolution of the New Right." Journal of American History. Vol. 96 No. 1: 123–148.

Turner, James Morton and Andrew Isenberg. 2018. *Republican Reversal: Conservatives and the Environment from Nixon to Trump.* Cambridge: Harvard University Press.

Turner, Tom. 2015. *David Brower: The Making of the Environmental Movement.* Berkeley: University of California Press.

Watson, Richard L. Jr., 1963. "The Defeat of Judge Parker: A Study in Pressure Groups and Politics." *The Mississippi Valley Historical Review.* Vol. 50 No. 2: 213–224.

Wellock, Thomas. 1992. "The Battle for Bodega Bay: The Sierra Club and Nuclear Power, 1958–1964." *California History.* Vol. 71.

Wellock, Thomas Raymond. 1996. *Critical Masses: Opposition to Nuclear Power in California: 1958–1978.* Madison: University of Wisconsin Press.

Wildavsky, Aaron. 1962. *Dixon-Yates: A Study in Power Politics.* New Haven: Yale University Press.

Wohlforth, Charles. 2010. *The Fate of Nature: Rediscovering our Ability to Save the Earth.* New York: St. Martin's Press.

Wolbrecht, Christina. 2000. *The Politics of Women's Rights: Parties, Position and Change.* Princeton: Princeton University Press.

Zaller, John R. 1992. *The Nature and Origins of Mass Opinion.* New York: Cambridge University Press.

Acknowledgments

I want to thank Jerry Taylor of the Niskanen Center, who commissioned a paper that got me started on this road. Joel Mabry was very helpful in coding party platforms and Jennifer Hadden offered sage advice on the environmental politics literature. Holly Burke and Sara Chieffo of the LCV provided data. Finally, I am grateful to series editor Frances Lee for seeing the potential in this project. This Element is in memory of my father Nathaniel Karol and my aunt Eleanor Glaser, who shared their love of nature with me.

Cambridge Elements

American Politics

Frances E. Lee
University of Maryland-College Park

Frances E. Lee is Professor of Government and Politics at the University of Maryland-College Park. She is author of Insecure Majorities: Congress and the Perpetual Campaign (2016), Beyond Ideology: Politics, Principles and Partisanship in the U.S. Senate (2009), and coauthor of Sizing Up the Senate: The Unequal Consequences of Equal Representation (1999).

About the Series

American Politics publishes authoritative contributions on American politics. Emphasizing works that address big, topical questions within the American political landscape, the series is open to all branches of the subfield and actively welcomes works that bridge subject domains. It publishes both original new research on topics likely to be of interest to a broad audience and state-of-the-art synthesis and reconsideration pieces that address salient questions and incorporate new data and cases to inform arguments.

Cambridge Elements ≡

American Politics

Elements in the Series

Policy Success in an Age of Gridlock: How the Toxic Substances Control Act was Finally Reformed
Lawrence S. Rothenberg
9781108628044

Roll Call Rebels: Strategic Dissent in the United States and United Kingdom
Justin H. Kirkland, Jonathan B. Slapin
9781108701556

Legislative Hardball: The House Freedom Caucus and the Power of Threat-Making in Congress
Matthew Green
9781108735810

Red, Green, and Blue: The Partisan Divide on Environmental Issues
David Karol
9781108716499

Contemporary US Populism in Comparative Perspective
Kirk Hawkins, Levente Littvay
9781108456821

A full series listing is available at: www.cambridge.org/core/series/elements-in-american-politics